SpringerBriefs in Computer Science

Series Editors

Stan Zdonik
Peng Ning
Shashi Shekhar
Jonathan Katz
Xindong Wu
Lakhmi C. Jain
David Padua
Xuemin Shen
Borko Furht
V. S. Subrahmanian
Martial Hebert
Katsushi Ikeuchi
Bruno Siciliano

Grega Jakus · Veljko Milutinović
Sanida Omerović · Sašo Tomažič

Concepts, Ontologies, and Knowledge Representation

 Springer

Grega Jakus
Sanida Omerović
Sašo Tomažič
Faculty of Electrical Engineering
University of Ljubljana
Ljubljana
Slovenia

Veljko Milutinović
School of Electrical Engineering
University of Belgrade
Belgrade
Serbia

ISSN 2191-5768   ISSN 2191-5776 (electronic)
ISBN 978-1-4614-7821-8   ISBN 978-1-4614-7822-5   (eBook)
DOI 10.1007/978-1-4614-7822-5
Springer New York Heidelberg Dordrecht London

Library of Congress Control Number: 2013939045

Printed on acid-free paper

Springer is part of Springer Science+Business Media (www.springer.com)

Contents

Chapter 1
Introduction

1.1 Introduction

The information world that we live in today presents us with a vast amount of data stored separately in books, newspapers, audio and video records of numerous different formats, internet and other media, all of them increasingly digitized. Moreover, there is an exponential increase in the number of these data, causing the capability of an average computer-literate person to find specific data or useful topic-related information to decrease rapidly. The negative impact these vast amounts of data have on finding relevant information could be partially alleviated by using efficient techniques for information structuring and retrieval. Popular search engines nowadays, however, still very often fail to retrieve documents relevant to the query. The algorithms of these search engines, namely, still mostly rely on keyword matching, regardless of the variety of individual meanings of the keywords, the complex meanings arising from the combinations of keywords into phrases, or even different meanings that occur when keywords and phrases are used in different contexts.

The introduced issues pose several fundamental questions: How can one efficiently extract the desired data from a huge data source? How does one find a necessary and potentially available, but unknown piece of information that represents the answer to a question or helps to resolve a problem? How complex must the underlying records be? It has been asserted that if the structure and function of all organisms that live or have lived on earth can simply be coded by triplet sequences of four nitrogenous base pairs A, G, T and C, there is no reason for a knowledge record to be more complex (Novak 2007). In addition, if further pursuing the analogy, we can shortly establish that merely recording knowledge is not enough. To be of immediate practical use, the recorded knowledge must be imbedded in an appropriate, highly reliable processing environment (such as the cell).

Knowledge, as usually presented, mostly appears either in an unstructured or non-uniformly structured way, making it unsuitable for further processing (think of, for example, the numerous related but incompatible computerized record systems present within every government department or business organization).

G. Jakus et al., *Concepts, Ontologies, and Knowledge Representation*,
SpringerBriefs in Computer Science, DOI: 10.1007/978-1-4614-7822-5_1,
© The Author(s) 2013

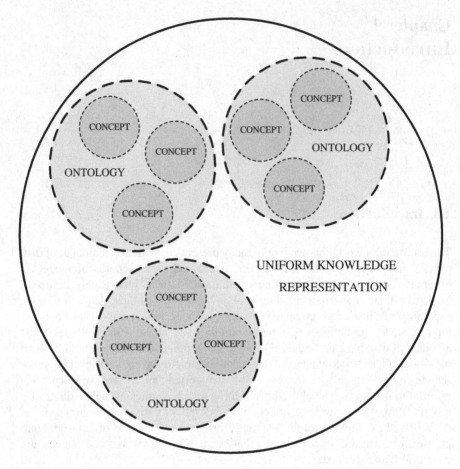

Fig. 1.1 Uniform knowledge representation consisting of ontologies populated by concepts

In this survey,[1] we follow a widespread general agreement among the majority of the cited authors that uniform knowledge representation should, in general, be achievable by using ontologies populated with concepts. The connection between concepts, ontologies and knowledge representation is illustrated in Fig. 1.1: concepts act as some sort of basic building blocks for ontologies, while the latter serve as the key elements of knowledge representation.

In order to express their thoughts in their everyday conversation, people use concepts although there is no unique definition of concept or a commonly accepted agreement of what a concept is. Nevertheless, we understand through observation how concepts are used in human communication to carry a specific, more or less defined meaning, for example: a house, a dog, a car, or some more abstract idea.

_____

[1] This survey contains excerpts from work related to concept modeling in multimedia applications (Omerovic et al. 2011).

We do not know how concepts are derived from everyday perception or acquired knowledge. For every person, concept derivation appears to be unique. Because of the importance of expressing specific delimited meanings in knowledge representation, the second chapter of this survey focuses on various approaches to concepts.

Concepts alone are not enough. Grouping related concepts into ontologies, as illustrated in Fig. 1.1, has proven to be an efficient way of organizing related concepts. Loosely stated, an ontology is a convenient means of uniting a subject, a relationship, and an object to talk about. The value of such organization lies especially in the fact that ontologies are intended for organizing concepts under a common specification in order to facilitate knowledge sharing. For example, we are able to present the abstract concept of a *person* by means of ontologies defined by the Web Ontology Language (OWL) (OWL 2009) with datatype properties such as *firstName, lastName, gender, birthday, homeAddress, officeAddress, email, cellPhone, fax, homepage*, etc. Such representation can be shared with other users and interpreted in the same, uniform way. Because ontologies thus enable meaning to be captured and shared in a uniform manner, they become the essence of successful knowledge representation. Therefore, the Chap. 3 of this survey is dedicated to different views on ontologies.

The final goal of every application of knowledge, regardless of the nature of the agents using it (be it human or software), is solving some sort of a problem. Sharing acquired domain knowledge with the aid of ontologies is, however, only half-way towards accomplishing this goal. Ontologies are, namely, in most cases merely models consisting of concepts that are relevant for describing the real world and, as such, do not inherently specify the mechanisms that determine how the represented knowledge should be used in practice. To be of practical use, the ontologies must, therefore, be embedded into a broader scope of *knowledge representation* that supplements the ontologies with the means for using these formal schemes in problem solving. Based on these facts, the fourth chapter of the survey addresses various forms of knowledge representation and their practical use in computer systems that show intelligent behavior normally observed in human users.

The survey concludes with a section dedicated to trends and outlook in the field of knowledge representation.

References

Novak J (2007) Private communication, 23 Jan 2007

Omerovic S, Babovic Z, Tafa Z, Milutinovic V, Tomazic S (2011) Concept modeling: from origins to multimedia. Multimed Tools Appl 51(3):1175–1200

OWL Working Group (2009) OWL 2 web ontology language document overview. W3C recommendation 27 October 2009. http://www.w3.org/TR/owl-overview. Accessed 25 Sep 2012

Chapter 2
Concepts

A concept is an entity of consciousness. We know a concept when we encounter one "in action", because it exceeds its stand-in descriptive label as a word, phrase or sentence. A concept might be a directly conceived or an intuited object of thought. In general, every object, issue, idea, person, process, place, etc., can generate a concept. Although concepts are an integral part of human cognition (or perhaps precisely because of this fact), their exact definition is fairly difficult. Various viewpoints and approaches to their explanation are presented in the first part of the present chapter. To be of any practical use for representing knowledge, concepts cannot appear in isolation, but must be associated with each other. Thus, in the continuation of the chapter, the most important formalisms for organizing concepts are presented along with the examples of organizations in actual applications. The main practical application of concepts is document retrieval based on the actual meaning referred to with the search phrase instead of the one based on (more or less) literal phrase matching. The last section of the chapter is dedicated to the topics related to concept-based search.

2.1 Definition

The term "concept" comes from Latin word *conceptum* ("that which is conceived"). Although the explanation of a concept has been a mainly philosophical matter ever since the ancient era, it is also a subject matter of psychology and linguistics. Throughout the centuries, many theories about the nature of concepts have been proposed, many times fundamentally contradicting each other. It all seems that when trying to explain what a "concept" is, only few things hold for certain—the most apparent definitely being the fact that the unique definition of a concept does not exist.

Despite the challenging explanation and the absence of a uniform definition, it is very often accepted that concepts are somehow connected with the process of human cognition. It is also commonly established that concepts are *abstract* and *universal*.

G. Jakus et al., *Concepts, Ontologies, and Knowledge Representation*,
SpringerBriefs in Computer Science, DOI: 10.1007/978-1-4614-7822-5_2,
© The Author(s) 2013

The abstractness of concepts arises from the fact that concepts do not enclose the specifics of or differences between the objects to which they apply. In this sense, all objects to which a concept applies (also referred to as "extensions" of concepts) are treated as indistinguishable from the respective concept. Because concepts apply to every object in their extension in the same way, they are considered universal.

The abstract nature of concepts does, however, not prejudice the nature of objects in a concept's extension. These objects can thus be abstract or concrete, real or imaginary, atomic or composed of other objects. A concept can be anything existing in the human mind or shared through human language and behavior, for example an action, a task, a strategy or way of thinking (Gomez-Perez and Corcho 2002).

These are merely some of many viewpoints from which one can define the nature of concepts. In the continuation of this subsection, we have chosen to present the most important concept definitions grouped by the criterion whether concepts are defined explicitly or implicitly.

2.1.1 Explicit Concept Definitions

2.1.1.1 Concepts in Philosophy

The beginner of the classical theory of concepts is the Greek philosopher Aristotle. In his "theory of definition", he defined a concept by using a pair of two concepts which he named *genus* (a kind, sort or family) and *differentia* (a distinguishing characteristic). According to his theory, the concept *"human"* is, for example, defined as a *"thinking animal"*. The *"animal"* corresponds to *genus* as it determines the family human belongs to and *"thinking"* corresponds to *differentia* as it distinguishes humans from other animals.

Philosophers Locke and Schopenhauer considered concepts to be abstractions of what is obtained by some sort of individual experience in the form of sensation and reflection (Locke 1690; Schopenhauer 1851). Besides the concepts abstracted from human experience (the so-called a posteriori concepts), the German philosopher Immanuel Kant also mentions another type of concepts: those that originate in the human mind (Kant 1800). Kant referred to these concepts as *pure* or *a priori* concepts or *categories*. Two examples of a priori concepts are the concepts of time and space.

Another German philosopher, Gottlob Frege, argued that a concept reflects the way in which we comprehend the world around us (Frege 1892). Frege gives an illustrative example which associates an object ("reference"), a symbol ("sign") and a concept ("sense") revealing the differences among them. The symbols *morning star* and *evening star* refer to the same object—planet Venus. However, the senses of these two terms are completely different, since the former is visible in the morning and the latter can be observed in the evening. The two symbols,

Fig. 2.1 The meaning
triangle

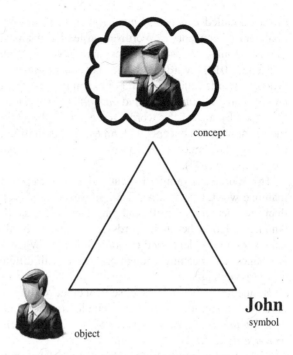

concept

John
symbol

object

therefore, represent two different concepts which correspond to different observations of the world, i.e. the time of observation in our particular example.

A similar explanation is given by John Sowa who considers a concept as a *"mediator that relates symbol to its object"* (Sowa 2000). Such mediation can be illustrated with the so-called meaning (or semiotic) triangle introduced by (Ogden and Richards 1923). In the lower two corners of the triangle in Fig. 2.1, there is an icon resembling a person named John and a printed symbol representing John's name. The cloud on the top represents a "neural excitation" that is induced by an object associated with the symbol representing the respective object. The "neural excitation" depicted in Fig. 2.1, for example, represents John working at his office and appears in one's mind when thinking about a person named John. This excitation, a mediator between the symbol and its object, is called a concept.

2.1.1.2 Concepts in Other Scientific Fields

In contrast to philosophy, where concepts are directly associated with the very essence of human existence and perception of the world, the treatment of concepts in other fields of science is often more pragmatic. There, the definitions are tailored to depend upon the way concepts are used in practice and are usually expressed in terms of the field's terminology.

In linguistics, a concept is most often considered as a unit of meaning formed through the abstraction of concrete words and phrases and as such corresponding to the so-called *conceptual meaning*. A good example illustrating the linguistic treatment of concepts is WordNet—a lexical database containing interconnected English nouns, verbs, attributes and adverbs (Miller 1995; Fellbaum 1998; Princeton 2010). WordNet defines concepts (although implicitly) through sets of synonym words called *synsets*. For example, a synset consisting of synonym words *homo*, *man*, *human being* and *human* defines a concept that can be lexically expressed by any of the words in the synset. In addition, WordNet complements such treatment of concepts with an explicit definition expressed in the description of the synset "concept" (*"an abstract or general idea inferred or derived from specific instances"*).

The WordNet example indicates that a concept can be represented with more than one word. On the other hand, however, individual words can represent more than one meaning as well, and can, therefore, stand for more than one concept. Another relation between words and concepts is also significant: concepts are language-independent, while words are not. When translating among different languages, the meaning, though expressed with different words, can be preserved to a large extent.

Beside the above-presented, several other readings of concepts in linguistics are identified in (Smith 2004). For example, a concept can also be understood as *"a meaning that is shared in common by the relevant terms [and/or] in minds of those who use these terms"*.

In the field of engineering, a concept is related with building models of entities from reality. From such a perspective, concepts can be defined as *"creatures of the computational realm which exists ... through their representations in software, in UML diagrams, XML representations, in systems of axioms"*, etc. (Smith 2004).

In contrast to engineering, a concept in mathematics transcends the reality that is recognized through our emotions and intuition. The mathematician Carl Benjamin Boyer defined mathematical concepts (such as the integral or derivative) as *"well-defined abstract mental constructs"* which are *"beyond the world of sensory experience ... although they may be suggested by observation of nature or intuition"* (Boyer 1959).

2.1.1.3 Concepts in Knowledge Representation

As already mentioned in the introduction, concepts are often considered as atomic elements in knowledge representations. Therefore, it is worth looking at how concepts are treated in this field.

One of the formalisms used to represent organized knowledge are concept maps. Here, concepts are defined as a *"perceived regularity in events or objects, or records of events or objects, designated by a label"* (Novak and Cañas 2008). The label for most concepts is a word or a symbol.

Description logic is a formalism for representing logic-based knowledge through concepts (classes), roles (relations) and individuals (objects). In description logic, concepts denote sets of individual objects (Baader and Nutt 2002).

Frames (described in Sect. 4.2.1.1) are knowledge representation structures influenced by the organization of human memory. In contrast to many other formalisms for representing knowledge, concepts are not considered as atomic units when represented with frames. Instead, they are treated as sets of highly structured entities which can be described with recursive structures consisting of pairs of attributes (called "slots" in frame terminology) and their values (Petersen 2007).

Closely related to frames are object-oriented languages. Object-oriented languages recognize two elemental structures: *classes* and their instances, referred to as *objects*. A class defines the properties and methods that can be used to manipulate the properties of all the objects that are instances of a particular class. The properties and methods defined in a class provide the objects with a state and behavior. As classes act as abstractions of concrete objects, they correspond to concepts while objects correspond to instantiations of concepts.

2.1.2 Implicit Concept Definitions

If concepts can be recognized, but cannot be defined exactly and consistently, how can a machine, for example, distinguish which words in a text represent concepts and which do not? Which terms carry more meaning than others? How can one make concepts recognizable, so that they can be automatically extracted from any type of texts?

A Vector Space Model (VSM) (Salton and Wong 1975) presents one possible answer for the above questions. In VSM, each document is represented as a vector with coordinates representing the frequency of the observed index terms in a document. The number of coordinates (the dimension) of each vector corresponds to the number of index terms observed in a document collection. For example, in Fig. 2.2, three different documents are represented by three two-dimensional index vectors, whereby the two dimensions correspond to two index terms observed in the documents.

A level of similarity between two documents can be measured by calculating the inner product of the corresponding index vectors or the inverse function of the angle between them (when the angle between two vectors is zero, the similarity function is at a maximum, and vice versa). The latter approach is also used in the example from Fig. 2.2.

The similarity among documents can also be measured when a new index term is assigned to a document collection. If the similarity level decreases, the newly assigned index term has a high discrimination value and is as such considered as a "good" index term. The opposite holds for a "bad" index term. Therefore, "good" index terms can be recognized as concepts, since they represent the smallest units of knowledge carrying as much meaning as possible (i.e. enough to decrease the similarity level between the documents when assigned to a document collection).

Fig. 2.2 Representing documents by two-dimensional vectors in the Vector Space

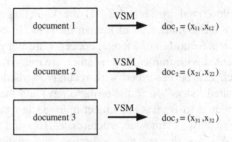

doc_i– vector representing i-th document

$x_{i,j}$ – value of occurence of j-th index term in i-th document ($0 \leq x_{i,j} \leq 1$)

$\lambda_{k,l}$ – angle between k-th and l-th vector ($0 \leq \lambda_{k,l} \leq 90°$)

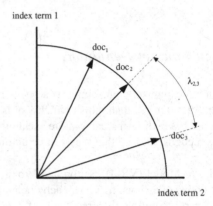

Figure 2.3 shows document representations when a "good" discriminating term is added to VSM. Before assigning the index term 3, the three document vectors reside on one plain formed by the axes of index terms 1 and 2 (Fig. 2.2). After adding the index term 3 to the document collection, a third dimension is added to vector space (Fig. 2.3). An additional coordinate is added to each of the three vectors and the angles between them are consequently increased.

More implicit definitions of concepts can be found, for example, in the field of word-sense disambiguation, especially in automatic identification of word senses (the so-called word-sense induction). For example, the approach to the word-sense induction known as *word clustering* involves grouping of semantically similar words. As such, they can reflect a specific meaning and can thus be considered as concepts. The determination of similarity between words can, for example, be based on the observation of the syntactic dependencies of particular words in actual texts (e.g. words acting as subjects of a verb, direct objects of a verb, adjectives of a noun etc.). In this manner, concepts can be implicitly defined as clusters of words that share a high amount of syntactic dependencies.

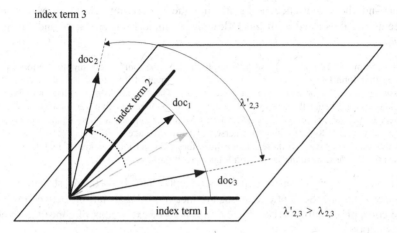

$$doc_1 = (x_{11}, x_{12}, x_{13})$$
$$doc_2 = (x_{21}, x_{22}, x_{23})$$
$$doc_3 = (x_{31}, x_{32}, x_{33})$$

Fig. 2.3 Document representations after assigning a new index term to the Vector Space Model

Beside the one presented, many other approaches and algorithms exist in the field (see, for example, the survey of (Navigli 2009)), but what they all have in common is clustering—the grouping of words representing distinct meanings. These clusters can be interpreted as concepts. The exact definition of a concept, however, varies depending on the definition of similarity that a particular method uses for grouping words.

This subsection presented several possible definitions of concepts. The next section discusses the issue of how concepts can be organized and thus be made predictably available for use.

2.2 Organization

For concepts to be of any practical use for representing knowledge, they cannot be isolated; on the contrary, they must be linked with each other. In the beginning of this section, we introduce the relations among concepts as the key means of organizing concepts. As the linking of concepts eventually results in the formation of graph-like structures, the second part of this section presents the most important formalisms for representing such graphical organizations of concepts. The section concludes with examples of some specific concept organizations, for example when concepts are used as application data in databases and for document indexing and retrieval.

2.2.1 Relationships Among Concepts

The richness of the relationships linking concepts used in every day communication and the importance of identifying the underlying relationships between
concepts are illustrated with the following example from Halladay and Milligan
(2004).

> The statement "John has an IQ of 150" explicitly describes only a very simple relationship
> (i.e., that John has some attribute named IQ that equals 150). However, the statement
> assumes a myriad of other implicit relationships. These relationships include mundane
> things like IQ being the acronym for Intelligence Quotient, or that 150 is a value that
> precedes 151 and is preceded by 149, or that John is commonly a human male name, or
> that an IQ equal to 150 indicates a person of above-average intelligence, etc. However,
> without the context of all these relationships, the statement looses some of its fidelity or
> meaning. In fact, meaning is the sum-total of relationships.

The basic means for organizing concepts into knowledge structures are
semantic relations. Semantic relations are meaningful associations between two or
more concepts or entities (i.e. objects, instances or extensions of concepts) (Khoo
and Na 2006).

The basic property of semantic relations is their *valence* (or "*arity*"), i.e. the
number of concepts a semantic relation can associate. The valence of a relation is
often expressed with the number of places, slots, fields or sides of the relation.
Most often, the relations are binary, connecting two concepts. The relation "*give*"
is, for example, a ternary relation, connecting the one who gives, the one who
receives and that which is given. The relations with valence higher than two can be
decomposed into binary relations. It was even suggested (Sowa 1984) that all
relations can, in fact, be presented as concepts linked with a single (and the most
primitive) "*link*" relation.

The quoted literature (e.g. Saussure 1916; Khoo and Na 2006; Stock 2010)
distinguishes between two basic types of semantic relations: paradigmatic and
syntagmatic relations. A *paradigmatic relation* is a relation between concepts that
is independent of the actual use of the respective concepts (e.g. their occurrence in
documents). For example, the concept "*guitar*" is inherently associated with the
concept "*musical instrument*" by the paradigmatic relation "*is a kind of*" (the
taxonomic relation). The hierarchical classification of paradigmatic relations is
presented in Fig. 2.4. On the other hand, a *syntagmatic relation* is a relation
between neighboring concepts in actual documents and as such, it only holds for
an "ad-hoc" association of concepts in a particular document. An example of a
syntagmatic relation is the relation "*play*" linking the concepts "*boy*" and "*guitar*"
in the sentence "*That boy plays the guitar*".

Some of the formalisms for concept organization, such as object-oriented
modeling languages and Semantic Web ontology languages, recognize a special
type of relation, referred to as *the attribute*. Attributes denote the properties of
concepts (or their extensions) and are usually represented as a feature of the entity

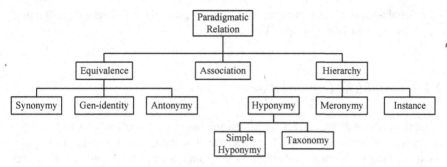

Fig. 2.4 The hierarchical classification of paradigmatic semantic relations (Stock 2010)

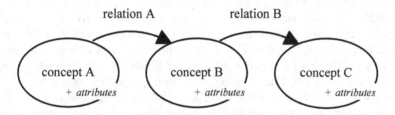

Fig. 2.5 The organization of concepts using relations and attributes

that is used to model concepts (or their extensions). Such representation of concepts using attributes in addition to semantic relations is illustrated in Fig. 2.5.

According to (Gomez-Perez and Corcho 2002), the attributes can be classified into the following four groups:

- *Class attributes* are assigned values that are attached to the concept and will therefore be the same for all instances of a concept.
- *Instance attributes* can be assigned different values for each instance (extension) of a concept.
- *Local attributes* are same-name attributes attached to different concepts.
- *Global attributes* can be applied to all concepts in a particular conceptual structure, for example, in an ontology.

The first two attribute types reflect the relationship between a concept and its instances. For example, the value of the attribute "chromosome number" appointed to the concept "human" is characteristic to all instances of this concept and can be thus considered a class attribute. On the other hand, the value of the attribute "age" is an instance attribute as it depends on a concrete person, for example, the next-door neighbor Susan, an instance of the concept "human".

The use of local and global attributes mainly depends on the representation requirements in actual applications. An example of a local attribute is the attribute "color". Although more diverse concepts within a particular conceptual structure can be related to this attribute, its value is local to a particular concept. An example of a global attribute is the attribute "description", which holds a verbal explanation for every concept in a conceptual structure.

2.2.2 Graphical Organizations

In general, the use of semantic relations for linking concepts results in the organization of concepts in a graph-like structure. The three most common formalisms for describing such graphical structures are *conceptual graphs*, *concept maps* and *semantic networks*.

A conceptual graph (Sowa 1984) contains two kinds of nodes: concepts and conceptual relations. In the conceptual graph in the Fig. 2.6, concepts are presented with rectangles, and conceptual relations are presented with circles. Every edge in the conceptual graph links a conceptual relation to a concept. In the graph in Fig. 2.6, the concept *read*, thus, has an *agent* in the form of a person named *John*; a *theme*, the thing that is the object of the activity, in this case a *book*; and the *place*, where the situation is taking place, in this case the *living room*.

Concept maps are comprised of concepts and relationships between concepts. The relationships are expressed with words or phrases indicated on the edges linking concepts as shown in Fig. 2.7. The concepts and relationships in concept maps form propositions, or meaningful statements, *"about some object or event in the universe, either naturally occurring or constructed"* (Novak and Cañas 2008). Concepts in concept maps are organized hierarchically with the most general concepts arranged at the top of the map and more specific concepts placed bellow. When the propositions in a concept map are represented in a formal, computer-interpretable way, a concept map turns into a *semantic network* (Cañas and Novak 2009).

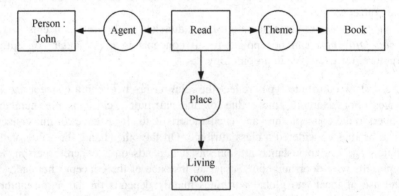

Fig. 2.6 Conceptual graph representing the proposition *"John is reading a book in the living room"*

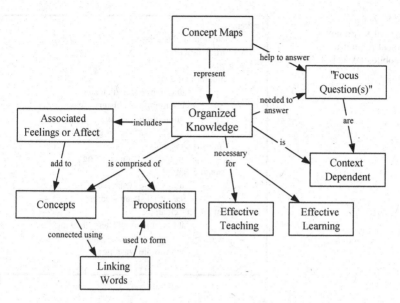

Fig. 2.7 A graphical organization of concepts in a concept map (Novak and Cañas 2008)

2.2.3 Specific Organizations of Concepts

2.2.3.1 Application Data in Databases

When intended to be used in actual applications, concepts are most often "stored" in computer databases and organized as data items together with respective cross-data relationships (Zellweger 2003). Some modeling techniques that follow the same approach are:

- entity-relationship model (Chen 1976),
- object-role modeling (Halpin 2006), and
- Unified Modeling Language (OMG 2012).

The above techniques share the same basic concept structure in which data items exhibit the associations among different neighboring data. The essence of grasping the meaning of the data in a database lies in the ability to assign an explanation to each of these associations, which provides a conceptual model for the application data (Zellweger 2003).

2.2.3.2 Indexing and Information Retrieval

Conceptual indexing offers one possible method of organizing concepts that are recognized in documents. The conceptual indexing method proposed by (Woods 1997) indexes phrases according to their conceptual structure instead of merely

Fig. 2.8 A fragment of a
conceptual taxonomy in a
document related to
automobiles (Woods 1997)

```
brokers
        automobile brokers
        truck brokers
cleaning
        automobile cleaning
                automobile steam cleaning
                automobile upholstery cleaning
                automobile washing
                        car washing
        industrial cleaning
                industrial steam cleaning
        steam cleaning
                automobile steam cleaning
                industrial steam cleaning
        upholstery cleaning
                automobile upholstery cleaning
        washing
                automobile washing
                car washing
```

indexing them alphabetically. Each conceptual structure represents the way to compose the meaning of a phrase by combining several atomic elements, i.e. concepts.

An example of a conceptually indexed document is presented in Fig. 2.8. After parsing a phrase into one or more conceptual structures, the indexing system classifies the phrase according to the generality of its meaning. Such classification is achieved by utilizing the knowledge on the generality of relationships among individual elements of the phrase. For example, by utilizing the knowledge that a *car* is a sort of *automobile* and that *washing* is a kind of *cleaning,* the indexing system can determine that the phrase "*car washing*" represents a type of "*automobile cleaning*".

Another practical example of conceptual indexing is a thesaurus—the listing of words with similar, related, or opposite meanings. The "Joint INIS/ETDE thesaurus" (IAEA 2007), for example, contains structured information about the concepts in science and technology. Each record in the thesaurus consists of three components:

- a descriptor, i.e. a term identifying a concept;
- bibliographic data identifying the term entry date and corresponding remarks; and
- interrelationship indicators between individual concepts in the thesaurus. Three types of interrelationship indicators can be assigned:

    - preferential indicators (e.g. "used for"—UF),
    - hierarchical indicators (e.g. "broader term"—BT or "narrower term"—NT), and
    - an affinitive indicator ("related term"—RT).

Fig. 2.9 An example from
the Joint INIS/ETDE
thesaurus

PLUTONIUM
1996-01-24
UF dymac system
UF dynamic materials accountability system
BT1 actinides
BT1 transuranium elements
NT1 plutonium-alpha
NT1 plutonium-beta
NT1 plutonium-delta
NT1 plutonium-epsilon
NT1 plutonium-gamma
RT nuclear fuels
RT plutonium recycle

An example of an entry from the Joint INIS/ETDE thesaurus is presented in Fig. 2.9. The first two lines of the entry contain the term descriptor and the date of entry, while the remaining lines contain the relationships to other entries. The number following the interrelationship indicator (e.g. BT1) indicates the level (depth) of the relationship.

Conceptual indexing can also be conducted by ordinary users when annotating their documents for their efficient future retrieval. The conceptual indexing method proposed by Voss et al. (1999) is based on the manual marking textual elements in documents that are relevant to the user and could, therefore, also be relevant to others. The indexed concepts are not defined formally, therefore they must be interpreted in the context of their occurrences in the documents. The marked concepts can be organized by using two simple relations:

- the "*comprise*" relation, used for grouping several concepts into a new concept, and
- the "*associated*" relation, used when two concepts are considered to be closely associated, but not necessarily grouped into another concept.

The organization of concepts intended for describing the visual content of images is presented in (Jörgensen et al. 2001). The proposed conceptual structure organizes the visual attributes into four syntactic and six semantic levels. The attributes in the syntactic levels describe how an image is composed by using basic techniques and building blocks such as dots, lines, patterns and colors. The syntactic levels include the following four groups of attributes:

- *Type/technique* level contains the attributes that specify the type of image or the technique that was applied to create the image (e.g. color photograph).
- *Global distribution* level includes the attributes that classify the image based on its overall content that is determined by identifying the low-level perceptual characteristics such as color and texture (e.g. grey, blue, clear).

- *Local structure* level is involved in the categorization of the individual components extracted from the image (e.g. dots, lines, tones, texture).
- *Composition* level describes the specific layout of the basic elements in the image (e.g. symmetry, center of interest, leading lines and viewing angle), which are otherwise identified at the local structure level.

The attributes on the semantic levels describe the meaning of the elements in the image:

- *Generic Objects* and *Generic Scene* levels contain the attributes that describe the objects (e.g. tree, child, car) and scenes (e.g. city, landscape, portrait, indoor, outdoor), both of which can be recognized by using common knowledge.
- *Specific Object* and *Specific Scene* levels refer to the named entities (e.g. Albert Einstein, Eiffel Tower) and scenes (e.g. Paris, Times Square, Central Park). A more specialized knowledge is required for the recognition of specific objects and scenes compared to their generic counterparts.
- Attributes at the *Abstract Object* and *Abstract Scene* levels are used to describe what the individual objects in the image depict (e.g. angry woman) and what theme is represented in the image (e.g. sadness, happiness). The description at the abstract level is very demanding because it requires very specialized or even interpretative knowledge. Such description is therefore very subjective, as the choice of attributes might differ significantly for different describers.

The conceptual structure consisting of the introduced levels can be represented in the form of a pyramid, as shown in Fig. 2.10. The pyramidal shape illustrates

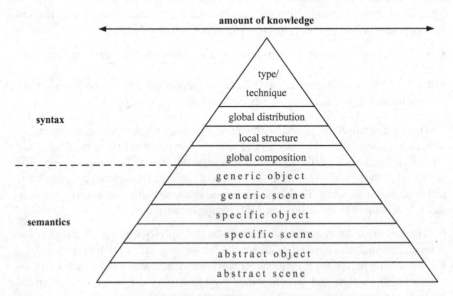

Fig. 2.10 Organizing concepts for describing the visual content in images based on the amount of knowledge needed for indexing (Jörgensen et al. 2001)

the volume of knowledge that is generally required for indexing images. The amount of knowledge required increases from the syntactic levels at the top to the semantic levels at the bottom of the pyramid. For example, to identify the individual objects in an image, more knowledge is required than to merely recognize the image type (e.g. color image). In addition, more knowledge is needed to identify a specific object or scene (e.g. face recognition, Central Park in New York City) than to recognize a generic object or scene (e.g. face detection, park).

The arrangement of attributes at various levels makes the model useful in many fields and for variety of indexing and retrieval methods. For example, the presented organization supports both automatic and manual indexing. Automatic indexing can be performed at syntactic levels where no specific world knowledge is required. On the other hand, the attributes at semantic levels used to categorize, describe and search for visual content can, in most cases, only be used by humans.

This section presented some general aspects of organizing concepts, including various forms of practical methods of organization applied to the fields of data storage, indexing and information retrieval. The following section is dedicated to the practical use of concepts organized in a uniform manner.

2.3 Concept Use

Various examples presented earlier in this chapter demonstrate that the same concepts can often be expressed by using different keywords. For example, if one says: "*I have a doctorate*" and "*I have a PhD*", these are two different statements, but they express the same concepts. In a typical searching scenario, the user is trying to retrieve the documents containing particular concepts of interest rather than exact keywords used in the query to refer to these concepts. As the concept-based search focuses on concepts rather than merely on words representing them, it presents a step ahead in the evolution of searching (Fig. 2.11). The concept-based search is, therefore, the main focus of this subsection related to concept use.

Three types of concept-based search systems are presented next: the Key-Concept is based on conceptual indexing, the Automated Generated Thesaurus

Fig. 2.11 Timeline of the searching evolution (Schatz 1997)

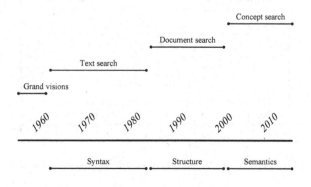

Approach provides alternate search terms in order to overcome the differences in terminology, and the Semantic Web search engines enable concept-based retrieval of the Semantic Web documents.

2.3.1 KeyConcept

The architecture of KeyConcept conceptual search engine is presented in Fig. 2.12 (Ravindran and Gauch 2004). In the indexing stage, the system applies conceptual indexing to the supplied documents. During the retrieval stage, the system ranks the indexed documents based on their similarity with the concepts (or the usual keywords) provided by the user.

The indexing process includes *classifier training* and *collection indexing*. In classifier training, the concepts in various sets of training documents are recognized and indexed by a traditional indexer using a modified *tf.idf* (*term frequency, inverse document frequency*) weighting method. The results of classifier training are vectors containing weighted terms representing distinct concepts that had been recognized during the training stage. The method for calculating weights is presented in Fig. 2.13. The weight of a term depends on (i) the frequency of the term's occurrence in the training documents for the particular concept the term represents, (ii) the rarity (or inversed frequency) of the term in the training documents for all concepts, and (iii) the frequency of the individual documents in the training set containing the term representing the particular concept.

During *collection indexing*, the conceptual indexer processes new documents using a Vector Space Model (Salton and Wong 1975) (see Sect. 2.1.2).

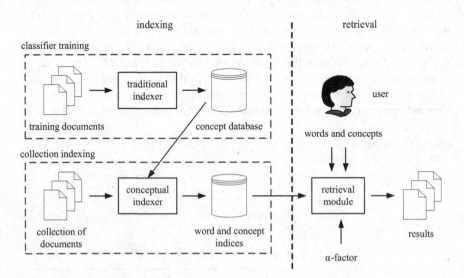

Fig. 2.12 The architecture of KeyConcept (Ravindran and Gauch 2004)

$$wt_{i,j} = tf_{i,j} * icf_i * cdf_{i,j}$$
$$icf_i = \log(n/cf_i)$$
$$cdf_{i,j} = \log(cdf_j/df_i)$$

$wt_{i,j}$ (term weight) = the weight of the term i representing the concept j
$tf_{i,j}$ (term frequency) = the frequency of term i in the training documents for concept j
icf_i (inverse concept frequency) = the rarity of the term i in the training sets for all concepts
$cdf_{i,j}$ (concept document frequency) = the frequency of the individual training documents in the training set
            containing the term i as a representative of the concept j

n = total number of concepts
cf_i = number of concepts containing term i
cdf_j = number of training documents for concept j
df_i = number of training documents containing term i

Fig. 2.13   The modified *tf.idf* weighting method used in KeyConcept

The supplied documents are classified by comparing their representative vectors to concept vectors that were computed in classifier training. The results of the collection indexing are indices that represent the similarity between a particular document in the collection and the concept vectors. The concept indices for each document are stored in the "word and concept index" (WCI) database which, as its name suggests, also contains standard word indices.

The retrieval is carried out by searching the WCI database for keywords or concepts that were provided by the user. The ranking of search results is computed by considering the relative importance of concept matching in relation to word matching, which is provided by the configurable α-factor.

2.3.2 Automated Generated Thesaurus Approach

Thesauri can be an efficient tool for concept-based retrieval in the text domain. The Automated Generated Thesaurus Approach (AGTA) (Chen et al. 1998) provides an ability to fine tune the keywords a user had (or should have had) in mind when forming a particular query. AGTA carries this out in several stages:

- *Document collection* includes collecting a set of documents in a subject domain serving as the thesaurus base.
- *Automatic indexing* involves the identification of terms (i.e. "*subject descriptors*") appearing in the document collection using the automatic indexing technique proposed by Salton (1989).
- In *co-occurrence analysis*, first term frequency (*tf*) and inverse document frequency (*idf*) are calculated (see Sect. 2.3.1). The two values are used to assign weights to each term in a document in order to represent the term's level of importance.

Cluster analysis then creates a network of terms with weighted connections, describing the similarity among terms.

- In the *associative retrieval* stage, the Hopfield algorithm (Hopfield 1982) is used to retrieve the terms that are related to the input term provided by the user. The algorithm first "activates" the neighbors of the input term, which are most strongly associated with the term itself. The algorithm then combines their weights and repeats the activation process on their neighbors. As the algorithm is iterative, this activation process "spreads" away from the input term and eventually fades away. The activation weights of the terms farther away from the input term are, namely, gradually decreasing and thus these terms are eventually excluded from the activation process.

Due to the fact that associative retrieval provides synonym terms or terms that have very similar meaning, these terms can be considered as representations of the same concept. The retrieved terms can thus be used to overcome vocabulary differences, for example in scientific information retrieval or in order to alleviate the problem of information overload when searching through huge information sources, such as the Web. For example, by using the terms suggested by the thesaurus, a user can enhance keyword-based web search to retrieve more relevant results.

2.3.3 Semantic Web

Before addressing the concept-based search on the Semantic Web, we shall briefly describe the latter. The Semantic Web (Berners-Lee et al. 2001) is the vision of Web of the future with the structure of information that is understandable to computers, so the latter can perform many tasks instead of humans, for example finding, sharing, and combining information. The technologies that constitute the Semantic Web are organized in the so-called Semantic Web stack. The stack with outlined key technologies is shown in Fig. 2.14.

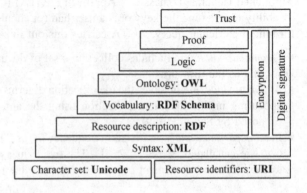

Fig. 2.14 The Semantic Web technology stack

The essence of the Semantic Web is *Resource Description Framework* (RDF) (RWG 2012a), a language for describing resources in the form of triplets. The triplets consist of a subject, an object and a predicate associating the former two. For example, the predicate "title" associates this book (the subject) with its title "Concepts, Ontologies, and Knowledge Representation" (the object).

The layers below the resource description layer provide the means to encode RDF triplets without imposing any semantic constraints on the selection of the subject, predicate and object.

- *eXtensible Markup Language* (XML) (W3C 2012), a language designed to transport and store data, provides the basic syntax for encoding the triplets. RDF documents recorded in the syntax of XML can easily be exchanged between computers and applications.
- The content in XML is encoded in Unicode standard that provides a character set for the representation of text in the majority of the presently used writing systems.
- The resources described by the RDF triplets can be any objects expressed with a *Uniform Resource Identifier* (URI) (Berners-Lee et al. 2005). URI is a string of characters that identifies a resource in a network.

The layers above the resource description layer comprise technologies that provide meaning to the RDF statements:

- RDF Schema (RWG 2012b) uses RDF language to define the basic application-specific vocabulary that is used for describing resources with the means of classes, subclasses and properties. The classes are often viewed as concepts, as they combine a set of individual resources (objects) with common properties.
- *Web Ontology Language* (OWL) (OWL 2009) extends the vocabulary of RDF Schema with the constructs that enable the description of more advanced relationships among the classes, thus enabling the construction of ontologies.

The upper three layers in the Semantic Web stack are not yet fully standardized and implemented. As such, they currently mostly represent the ideas that are supposed to be realized in order to entirely implement the Semantic Web. These layers include:

- the Logic layer containing the means to make inferences based on knowledge represented in ontologies;
- the Proof layer that executes the rules defined in the Logic layer; this layer enables the drawing of conclusions from given sets of facts and thus acquiring new knowledge from the knowledge already adopted; and
- the Trust layer containing the decision making mechanisms to differentiate whether to trust the given proof from the bottom layers. In addition, the mechanisms of cryptography, such as digital signature and encryption, may also be used to ensure privacy and verify that the Semantic Web statements originate from a trusted source.

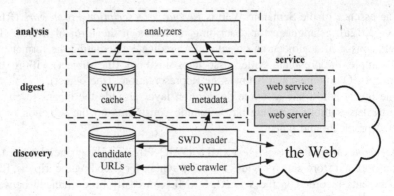

Fig. 2.15 The architecture of the Semantic Web search engine Swoogle (Finin et al. 2005)

Semantic Web technologies enable searching that is not limited merely to keyword matching, but can in fact be based on concepts. Examples of such Semantic Web search engines include GoPubMed (Doms and Schroeder 2005; GoPubMed 2012), *Semantic Web Search Engine* (SWSE) (Hogan et al. 2011; SWSE 2012; hakia 2012; Watson 2012; Sindice 2012) and Swoogle (Ding et al. 2004; Finin et al. 2005).

The architecture of Swoogle, for example, comprises several components (Fig. 2.15):

- The *discovery component* consists of *crawlers* that discover candidate *Uniform Resource Locators* (URLs) referencing *Semantic Web Documents* (SWDs). SWDs are all documents containing the RDF triplets.
- The *digest component* caches SWDs from the Web. The component then creates their corresponding metadata as well as the metadata describing individual concepts (also referred to as SWTs—Semantic Web Terms) contained in the SWDs. In addition, this component also identifies the relations among individual SWDs and SWTs.
- The main task of the *analysis component* is to classify and rank the cached SWDs and SWTs by their importance. The ranking algorithm used by Swoogle is a modified version of Google's PageRank algorithm (Page et al. 1999), adapted to account for the semantics of links in SWDs.

Searching for SWDs and their relationships with other SWDs and SWTs is possible through the web interface (Swoogle 2012) as well as through web services.

Although concepts and ontologies as such are presented in separate layers in the Semantic Web technology stack, in practice there is often no clear distinction where the use of uniformly organized concepts stops and the use of ontologies begins. The criteria for classifying the organization of concepts in an ontology are discussed in the next chapter.

References

Baader F, Nutt W (2002) Basic description logics. In: Baader F et al (eds) The description logic handbook. Cambridge University Press, Cambridge, pp 47–100

Berners-Lee T, Hendler J, Lassila O (2001) The semantic web. Sci Am 284(5):34–43

Berners-Lee T, Fielding R, Masinter L (2005) Uniform resource identifier (URI): generic syntax, RFC 3986. http://tools.ietf.org/html/rfc3986. Accessed 25 Sep 2012

Boyer CB (1959) The history of the calculus and its conceptual development. Courier Dover Publications, New York

Cañas AJ, Novak JD (2009) What is a concept map? http://cmap.ihmc.us/docs/conceptmap.html. Last update 28 Sep 2009. Accessed 25 Sep 2012

Chen H, Houston AL, Sewell RR, Schatz BR (1998) Internet browsing and searching: user evaluation of category map and concept space techniques. J Am Soc Inform Sci 49(7):582–603

Chen PP (1976) The entity-relationship model—toward a unified view of data. ACM Trans Database Syst 1(1):9–36

Ding L, Finin T, Joshi A, Pan R, Cost RS, Peng Y, Reddivari P, Doshi VC, Sachs J (2004) Swoogle: a search and metadata engine for the semantic web. In: Proceedings of the thirteenth ACM international conference on information and knowledge management, Washington, DC, Nov 2004

Doms A, Schroeder M (2005) GoPubMed: exploring PubMed with the gene ontology. Nucleic Acids Res 33:783–786

Fellbaum C (ed) (1998) WordNet: an electronic lexical database. MIT Press, Cambridge

Finin T, Ding L, Pan R, Joshi A, Kolari P, Java A, Peng Y (2005) Swoogle: searching for knowledge on the semantic web. In: Proceedings of the national conference on artificial intelligence (AAAI), Pittsburgh, 2005

Frege G (1892) Über Sinn und Bedeutung. In: *Zeitschrift für Philosophie und philosophische Kritik*. English edition: Frege G (1980) On Sense and Reference (trans: Black M). In: Geach P, Black M (eds) *Translations from the Philosophical Writings of Gottlob Frege*, 3rd edn. Blackwell, Oxford

Gomez-Perez A, Corcho O (2002) Ontology languages for the semantic web. IEEE Intell Syst 17(1):54–60

GoPubMed® (2012) http://www.gopubmed.org. Accessed 25 Sep 2012

hakia.com (2012) http://www.hakia.com/. Accessed 25 Sep 2012

Halladay S, Milligan C (2004) The application of network science principles to knowledge simulation. In: Proceedings of the 37th annual Hawaii international conference on system sciences, Big Island, 5–8 Jan 2004

Halpin T (2006) Object-role modeling (ORM/NIAM). In: Bernus P, Mertins K, Schmidt G (eds) Handbook on architectures of information systems. International handbooks on information systems. Springer, Heidelberg, pp 81–103

Hogan A, Harth A, Umbrich J, Kinsella S, Polleres A, Decker S (2011) Searching and browsing linked data with SWSE: the semantic web search engine. J Web Semant 9(4):365–401

Hopfield J (1982) Neural networks and physical systems with emergent collective computational abilities. Proc Natl Acad Sci USA 79(8):2554–2558

International Atomic Energy Agency (2007) Joint thesaurus, Part I + II. ETDE/INIS joint reference series no. 1 (Rev. 2). http://www-pub.iaea.org/MTCD/publications/PDF/JRS1r2_web.pdf. Accessed 25 Sep 2012

Jörgensen C, James A, Benitez AB, Chang SF (2001) A conceptual framework and empirical research for classifying visual descriptors. J Am Soc Inf Sci Technol 52(11):938–947

Kant I (1800) Logik. English edition: Kant I (1988) Logic (trans: Hartman RS, Schwarz W). Dover Publications, Mineola

Khoo C, Na J-C (2006) Semantic relations in information science. Annu Rev Inform Sci Technol 40(1):157–228

Locke J (1690) An essay concerning human understanding. Oxford University Press, New York, (1975)

Miller GA (1995) WordNet: a lexical database for English. Commun ACM 38(11):39–41

Navigli R (2009) Word sense disambiguation: a survey. ACM Comput Surv 41(2). doi: 10.1145/1459352.1459355

Novak J, Cañas A (2008) The theory of underlying concept maps and how to construct them. Technical report IHMC CmapTools 2006-01 Rev 01-2008, Florida Institute for Human and Machine Cognition

Ogden CK, Richards IA (1923) The meaning of meaning. Harcourt, Brace & Co, New York

Object Management Group (2012) UML® resource page. http://www.uml.org/. Accessed 25 Sep 2012

OWL Working Group (2009) OWL 2 web ontology language document overview. W3C recommendation 27 October 2009. http://www.w3.org/TR/owl-overview/. Accessed 25 Sep 2012

Page L, Brin S, Motwani R, Winograd T (1999) The PageRank citation ranking: bringing order to the web. Technical report, Stanford InfoLab

Petersen W (2007) Representation of concepts as frames. In: Skilters J, Toccafondi F, Stemberger G (eds) Complex cognition and qualitative science. The baltic international yearbook of cognition, logic and communication, vol 2. University of Latvia Press, pp 151–170

Princeton University (2010) About WordNet. http://wordnet.princeton.edu. Accessed 25 Sep 2012

Ravindran D, Gauch S (2004) Exploiting hierarchical relationships in conceptual search. In: Proceedings of the thirteenth ACM international conference on information and knowledge management, Washington, DC, 2004

RDF Working Group (2012) RDF—semantic web standards. http://www.w3.org/RDF/. Accessed 25 Sep 2012

RDF Working Group (2012) RDF vocabulary description language 1.0: RDF Schema (RDFS). http://www.w3.org/2001/sw/wiki/RDFS. Accessed 25 Sep 2012

Salton G (1989) Automatic text processing: the transformation, analysis, and retrieval of information by computer. Addison-Wesley, Reading

Salton G, Wong A (1975) A Vector Space model for automatic indexing. Commun ACM 18(11):613–620

Saussure F de (1916) Cours de linguistique générale. English edition: Saussure F de (1983) Course in General Linguistics (trans: Harris R). Open Court, La Salle

Schatz B (1997) Information retrieval in digital libraries: bringing search to the net. Science 275(5298):327–334

Schopenhauer A (1851) Parerga and paralipomena. English edition: Schopenhauer A (1974) Parerga and paralipomena: short philosophical essays (trans: Payne EFJ). Oxford University Press, New York

Sindice—the semantic web index (2012) http://www.sindice.com/. Accessed 25 Sep 2012

Smith B (2004) Beyond concepts: ontology as reality representation. In: Varzi AC, Vieu L (eds) Proceedings of the international conference on formal ontology and information systems, Turin, 4–6 Nov, pp 73–84

Sowa JF (1984) Conceptual structures: information processing in mind and machine. Addison-Wesley Publishing, Reading

Sowa JF (2000) Ontology, metadata, and semiotics. In: Conceptual structures: logical, linguistic, and computational issues. Lecture notes in computer science, vol 1867. Springer, Berlin, pp 55–81

Stock WG (2010) Concepts and semantic relations in information science. J Am Soc Inf Sci Tec 61(10):1951–1969

Swoogle Semantic Web Search Engine (2012) http://swoogle.umbc.edu/. Accessed 25 Sep 2012

SWSE—Semantic Web Search Engine (2012) http://swse.deri.org/. Accessed 25 Sep 2012

Voss A, Nakata K, Juhnke M (1999) Concept indexing. In: Proceedings of the international ACM SIGGROUP conference on Supporting group work, Phoenix, 14–17 Nov 1999, pp 1–10

W3C (2012) Extensible Markup Language (XML). http://www.w3.org/XML/. Accessed 25 Sep 2012

Watson Semantic Web Search (2012) http://kmi-web05.open.ac.uk/WatsonWUI/. Accessed 25 Sep 2012

Woods W (1997) Conceptual indexing: a better way to organize knowledge. Technical report, Sun Microsystems, Mountain View

Zellweger P (2003) A knowledge-based model to database retrieval. In: Proceedings of the international conference on integration of knowledge intensive multi-agent systems, Boston, 30 Sep–4 Oct 2003, pp 747–753

Chapter 3
Ontologies

The term "ontology" originates in philosophy, where it refers to the study of being or existence and the organization of reality (Guarino and Giaretta 1995; Studer et al. 1998). The term was introduced into engineering through the field of artificial intelligence where it refers to the representation of the real world in computer programs.

Ontology can be understood as a manner of organizing related concepts, as illustrated in Fig. 3.1. Such grouping of concepts has a more specifically defined purpose when compared to general organizations of concepts presented in previous section. The value of ontologies lies especially in the fact that ontologies are intended for organizing concepts under a common specification, often covering a complete domain, in order to facilitate knowledge sharing. The key properties of ontologies are often indicated directly in their definition, which is given in the following section.

3.1 Definition

The term ontology, similarly to the term concept, has been defined from many different viewpoints and with different degrees of formality. Ontologies can be viewed as mediators in the representation of knowledge by means of concepts. Therefore, ontologies lie between concepts (which they subsume) on the one hand and the embracing knowledge domain (within which they are embedded) on the other. Among several proposed definitions that explain ontology in the context of computer science, we prefer the following:

An ontology is a formal and explicit specification of a shared conceptualization.

The definition is coined from two widely adopted definitions provided by Tom Gruber (Gruber 1993) and Willem Borst (Borst 1997). In our opinion, the presented definition is important because it contains the following key aspects of ontologies (Studer et al. 1998):

G. Jakus et al., *Concepts, Ontologies, and Knowledge Representation*,
SpringerBriefs in Computer Science, DOI: 10.1007/978-1-4614-7822-5_3,
© The Author(s) 2013

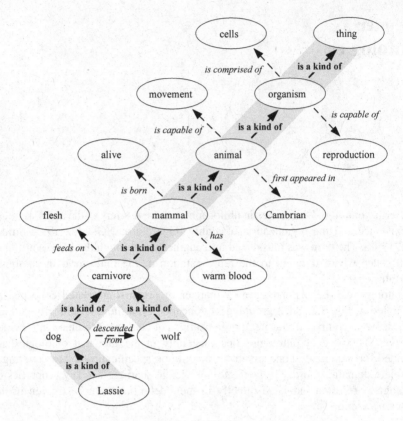

Fig. 3.1 An example of ontology with a highlighted taxonomical structure

- Ontologies are *conceptualizations*. They are abstract models consisting of concepts that are relevant for describing the real world. As such, ontologies act as a sort of surrogate of reality.
- Ontologies are *explicit*, by which we mean that concepts, relations and other components of ontology are defined explicitly.
- Ontologies are *formal* as they are intended to be processed by the computers. The use of natural language is not appropriate due to its ambiguousness, inconsistency and incomplete specification.
- Ontologies are *shared* as they capture consensual knowledge established by a group of interested users. Consequently, by choosing a specific ontology, the user makes a commitment to a set of terms, or *ontological commitments*, which determine how and what to perceive in the reality.

Knowledge sharing is actually one of the key roles of ontologies in computer science. In addition, combined with ontological commitments, the task of knowledge sharing differentiates ontologies from data models which are mostly intended to be used within a single application (Schreiber 2008).

3.2 Organization

Before constructing an ontology, some issues regarding the structure and content of ontologies have to be addressed. Firstly, one needs to choose the proper means to adequately describe a domain by selecting the relevant components of the domain model. Another matter to consider when building an ontology, is the level of its generality and, consequently, the level of its reusability. Finally, the ontology has to be constructed—manually, semi-automatically or even completely automatically. The presented options are the focus of this section.

3.2.1 Ontology Components

The components of ontologies typically include (Studer et al. 1998; Gomez-Perez and Corcho 2002; Navigli et al. 2003; Khoo and Na 2006):

- concepts, classes, collections, sets or types;
- objects, individuals, instances or entities;
- attributes, properties, or features of concepts or objects;
- attribute values;
- relations among classes and/or objects.

Ontology is typically built on top of a *taxonomy*—a hierarchical structure of concepts which limits the relation among the concepts to the formulation "*is a kind of*". Ontology builds on taxonomy by adding a richer network of semantic relations and additional components such as functions, restrictions or constraints, inference rules and axioms. Figure 3.1 shows an example of ontology with its taxonomical framework highlighted. This framework, formed by associating concepts using the relation "*is a kind of*", is further enriched with other semantic relations represented with dashed arrows and italic text.

3.2.2 Types of Ontologies

The definition of ontologies presented in the previous section represents them as a sort of conceptualizations of reality. The definition does not attempt to specify the level of generality of such a conceptualization and neither its scope. To provide an efficient reuse of ontologies and to avoid developing new ontologies when they are already available, it is, nevertheless, useful to divide ontologies in at least two levels of generality.

Generic ontologies (also referred to as *general, upper, foundation, top-level, common* or *core* ontologies) contain knowledge that can be reusable across various domains. The terms and descriptions from the vocabulary of generic ontologies describe very general and domain-independent concepts, such as events, time, space, matter, objects, actions, processes, causality and behavior. Examples of generic ontologies are Cyc (Lenat and Guha 1989; OpenCyc 2012), Dublin Core (DCMI 2012), *Suggested Upper Merged Ontology* (SUMO) (SUMO 2012) and *Descriptive Ontology for Linguistic and Cognitive Engineering* (DOLCE) (Gangemi et al. 2002; LAO 2012).

Specific ontologies represent concepts in a way that is specific to a particular domain, application, task, activity, method, etc. The exact subcategorization within this type of ontologies often depends on a particular field (e.g. knowledge engineering, natural language processing, information retrieval, etc.). In addition, more than one type of specific ontologies can be involved when addressing a particular problem. For example, Guarino (1998) suggested that three distinct specific types of ontology can be involved in building "ontology-driven information systems" (a term by which he referred to all ontology application areas within computer science).

The proposed hierarchical organization of ontologies to be used in ontology-driven information systems consists of domain, task and application ontologies, in addition to the top-level ontology (Fig. 3.2). The vocabularies of domain and task ontologies contain, respectively, the terms representing concepts of a particular domain (e.g. medicine) and a task or an activity (e.g. diagnosing a patient). The concepts in both types of ontologies are specialized from the top-level ontology. Application ontologies, in general, contain subsets of concepts from domain and task ontologies intended to be used in a specific application.

3.2.3 Languages, Tools and Methods for Organizing Ontologies

Ontologies are commonly encoded by using dedicated formal languages which are referred to as *ontology languages*. Ontology languages allow the sharing of knowledge and at the same time support its processing by providing reasoning rules.

Fig. 3.2 Types of ontologies in an ontology-driven information system (Guarino 1998)

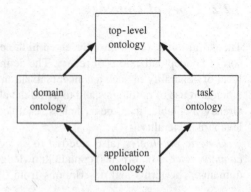

Generally speaking, ontology languages can be classified into two groups depending on the system of logic a particular language is based on. The ontology languages based on *description logic* traditionally originate from the field of artificial intelligence. Two typical examples of such languages are KL-ONE (Brachman and Schmolze 1985) and LOOM (MacGregor and Bates 1987). The other group of ontology languages, based on *first-order logic*, includes CYCL (Lenat and Guha 1989), KIF (Genesereth and Fikes 1992), Ontolingua (Gruber 1993) and Common Logic (CLWG 2012).

In the past fifteen years, a new family of ontology languages was created with the purpose of knowledge sharing on the internet. Examples of these languages include *XML-based Ontology exchange Language* (XOL) (Karp et al. 1999), *Simple HTML Ontology Extension* (SHOE) (Heflin et al. 1999), *Ontology Interchange Language* (OIL) (Fensel et al. 2001) and *Web Ontology Language* (OWL) (OWL 2009).

In addition to using the above-mentioned languages, ontologies can also be represented by conceptual graphs and semantic networks.

Ontologies can be created manually using dedicated software tools or automatically from various existing information resources. Some of the well-known software tools for creating ontologies include TERMINAE (Biebow et al. 1999; TERMINAE 2012), Protégé (Noy et al. 2001; Protégé 2012), KAON (Bozsak et al. 2002; KAON2 2012), DogmaModeler (DM 2012), HOZO (Mizoguchi et al. 2007; HOZO 2012) and OntoStudio (Weiten 2009; Semafora 2012). The methodology for constructing ontologies (also implemented in some of these tools) was developed under the projects OntoClean (Guarino and Welty 2002; OntoClean 2012), On-To-Knowledge (Sure and Studer 2002) and Dogma (Jarrar and Meersman 2002).

Beside the methodology and tools for manual generation of ontologies, several approaches to automatic or semi-automatic ontology generation (also referred to as "ontology learning") from existing resources have also been developed. The resources include:

- text documents (Kietz et al. 2000; Blaschke and Valencia 2002; Fortuna et al. 2007; Navigli et al. 2003);
- web documents (Maedche and Staab 2001; Gal et al. 2004; Navigli and Velardi 2004; Liu et al. 2005); and
- multimedia (Jaimes and Smith 2003).

A more thorough review of the established as well as more recent approaches to ontology construction can be found in the survey of (Barforoush and Rahnama 2012). The present survey, however, continues with examples on the practical use of ontologies.

3.3 Ontology Use

The primary purpose of the effort to define and organize ontologies is to facilitate knowledge sharing. Among numerous cases of use for ontologies, we have chosen to present their application in software agents, natural language processing, media annotation and knowledge extraction.

3.3.1 Software Agents

Software agents are computer programs acting on behalf of human users or other programs. A software agent that has the ability to acquire or apply knowledge to accomplish its goals is referred to as an *intelligent agent*. In this section we give examples of using ontologies to support intelligent agents in pervasive computing environments and Semantic Web services.

3.3.1.1 Intelligent Agents in Pervasive Computing Environments

In pervasive computing environments, agents cooperate with each other and with other devices and services in order to support human activity, goals and needs in an *"anywhere, anytime fashion"* (Chen et al. 2003a). For example, the architecture of the pervasive computing environment proposed in Chen et al. (2003b) is focused around an intelligent agent referred to as Intelligent Context Broker (ICB). The task of an ICB is to establish and share a coherent model of the environment it has been put in, including other devices, agents and people. After the ICB acquires information from sensors, devices and other agents in its environment, it integrates the information from various sources into a coherent model which is eventually used for reasoning and shared with other agents.

The proposed architecture is implemented by using a set of ontologies that provide concepts relevant for modeling pervasive computing environments (Chen et al. 2003a). A part of the ontology supporting the task of an ICB is presented in Fig. 3.3. The ontology is used to model a situation in which a speaker gives an invited speech or a presentation at a meeting which takes place in a particular room in a building. Beside the speaker, the room also hosts other participants representing the audience. The ontology also provides classes that represent environmental agents which are, according to the ontology, responsible for providing environmental information, such as whether a particular room is hosting an event, which specific people are participating in the event and what their intentions are.

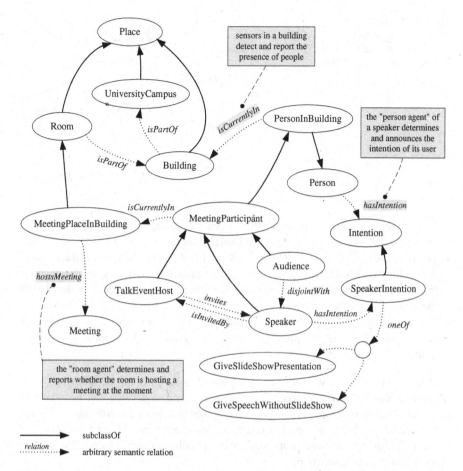

Fig. 3.3 A part of the ontology supporting the intelligent context broker (Chen et al. 2003a)

3.3.1.2 Semantic Web Services

The role of software agents on the Web is to implement web services—i.e. pieces of software that can communicate over the internet and provide functionalities that can be (re)used in web applications. Intelligent software agents and automated services which they provide to web users or other agents are crucial for the implementation of Semantic Web. In order to provide a shared vocabulary supporting the communication among the agents, the *OWL for Services* (OWL-S) ontology was specified (Martin et al. 2004). This ontology uses the OWL language to supplement the existing standards with explicit semantics enabling agents to automatically discover services and their capabilities, to invoke, monitor and compose these services, and to enable their interoperation. The OWL-S ontology is comprised of three lower-level ontologies (Fig. 3.4):

Fig. 3.4 Top level of the
OWL-S ontology for
describing semantic web
services (Martin et al. 2004)

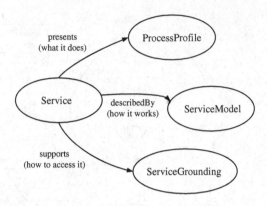

- The *profile ontology* ("ProcessProfile") describes what a service does and it is as such used for advertising and discovering services.
- The *process model ontology* ("ServiceModel") describes how a service is used. It provides the descriptions of how to interact with the service at the abstract level, the outcomes of using a specific service and the conditions under which the desired outcome will occur.
- The *grounding ontology* ("ServiceGrounding") specifies how to interact with a service via messages by providing concrete details such as message format, transport protocol, etc.

The way in which a web service is supposed to be used can be described with no more than one process model. On the other hand, a service can be assigned multiple alternative profiles and groundings, which allows advertising and inter-acting with the service in different contexts. As an example, Fig. 3.5 presents the most important classes and properties of the profile ontology. According to this ontology, a profile consists of:

- properties that link a profile instance to an instance of the corresponding service;
- human-readable information, such as service name, the contact information of the person responsible and textual description of the service; and
- description of functionality by specifying service inputs, outputs, parameters, preconditions and results, all of which are otherwise defined in the process model ontology.

3.3.2 Natural Language Processing

In the field of natural language processing, a general agreement holds that, whenever dealing with the meaning of texts, ontology should be involved. Ontology is considered as a resource of knowledge about the world (or a domain) consisting of primitive symbols, used for the representation of meaning.

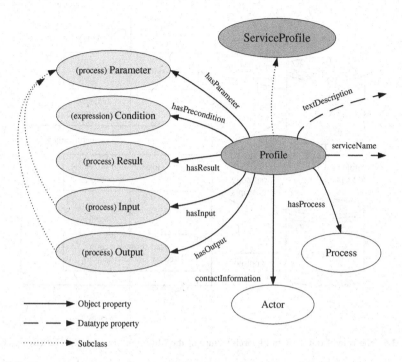

Fig. 3.5 The structure of the top level of the OWL-S profile ontology (Martin et al. 2004)

These symbols stand for concepts which are further interconnected with taxonomic ("*is-a-kind-of*"), semantic and discourse pragmatic relations (Mahesh 1996).

A typical system making use of an ontology is Mikrokosmos (Beale et al. 1995), an analyzer of source texts, which produces a *text meaning representation* (TMR) as the result of the analysis. TMR structures are natural language independent ("interlingual") representations of meaning and can, as such, theoretically be used as the basis for the generation of text in any target natural language.

Figure 3.6 presents the architecture of the Mikrokosmos analyzer and the role of ontology within the system. The analysis is twofold:

- the *syntactic analysis* involves determining syntactic functions and relations among and within particular words in the source text; while
- the *semantic analysis* involves generating TMRs by selecting word meanings which best suit the semantic restrictions from the ontology and lexicon.

The ontology in Mikrokosmos system has the following functions:

- It provides a permanent set of concepts used to represent meaning (Fig. 3.6a). The same set of concepts is expressed in different languages with the help of words from language-specific lexicons.
- It provides the basic building blocks to generate TMR structures (Fig. 3.6b). TMRs are constructed by instantiating the concepts from the ontology, and

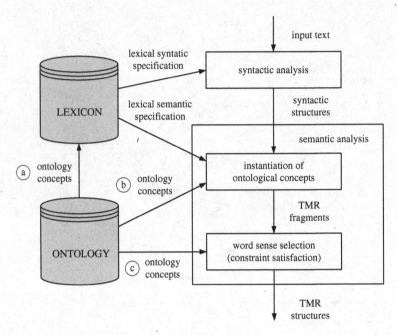

Fig. 3.6 The role of ontology in the architecture of the Mikrokosmos text analyzer (Beale et al. 1995)

supplementing the instances with additional linguistic information, such as aspects, attitudes or modalities.

- It provides constraints for the selection of semantic relations between concepts, which is especially useful for resolving ambiguities (Fig. 3.6c).
- It enables inferences, which can also be used for resolving ambiguities (Fig. 3.6c). In addition, inferences can also be used for filling in the missing textual meaning and for dealing with metonymies, metaphors and complex nominal phrases.

Figure 3.7 presents the taxonomic hierarchy of concepts on the first three levels of the Mikrokosmos ontology.

In the section concerning the methods of constructing ontologies, we mentioned that, among others, ontologies can be constructed automatically from various resources including text documents. Due to the fact that such a method of construction requires techniques of natural language processing supported by ontologies, we present one of the approaches, i.e. OntoLearn.

OntoLearn (Navigli et al. 2003) is a system for ontology learning from textual documents. It consists of the following processes (Fig. 3.8):

- *Extraction of domain terminology.* The language processor first extracts the candidate terms for domain terminology from the domain corpus. The terms are then filtered according to the specificity to a particular domain. The specificity is

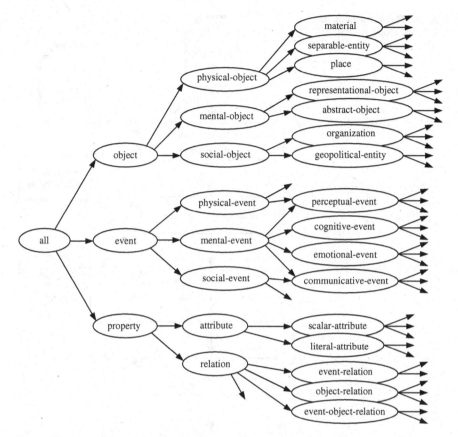

Fig. 3.7 Top-level hierarchy of the Mikrokosmos ontology (Mahesh 1996)

measured in the frequencies of candidate term across different domains, which are calculated with the aid of contrastive corpora.

- *Semantic interpretation.* Semantic interpretation involves finding the sense (concept) behind each component of a complex term. This is achieved by associating each of the term components to the corresponding concept in a generic ontology derived from WordNet.
- *Identification of taxonomic and semantic relations.* The concepts that were recognized in semantic interpretation are interlinked with taxonomic (*"is-a-kind-of"*) and other semantic relations, which generates a *"domain concept forest"*.
- *Ontology integration.* This process includes creating a specialized domain ontology by extending the generic ontology with the *"domain concept forest"* and removing the concepts that are not considered relevant to the domain.

Besides ontology learning, another practical use of OntoLearn is the translation of multi-word terminology. As the process of semantic interpretation relates individual terms of the compound term to the corresponding concepts (and

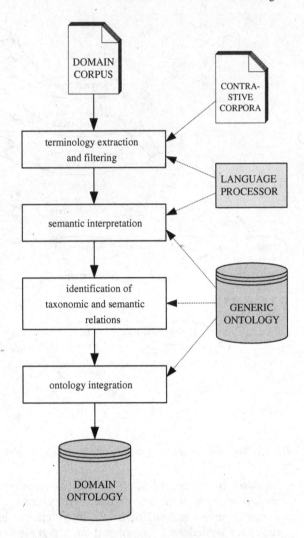

Fig. 3.8 The architecture of OntoLearn (Navigli et al. 2003)

consequently the whole compound term to a compound concept), this resolves the potential ambiguities in the source term. Two terms in different languages that can be matched to the same concepts can be considered mutual translations.

3.3.3 Media Content Annotation

The primary purpose of annotating different types of media, such as text, photos, audio or video, is to describe its content in order to facilitate the content retrieval process. To provide a shared vocabulary for such descriptions, once again, the use ontologies turn out to be a suitable choice. An example of an ontology used for photo annotation is described in Schreiber et al. (2001). The ontology consists of two parts: a photo annotation ontology and subject matter vocabulary.

The photo annotation ontology specifies the organization (template) for photo annotations, which is independent of a particular domain. It consists of the following features:

- A *subject matter feature* is used to describe the subject a photo depicts. The subject matter feature links photo annotation ontology to the subject matter vocabulary.
- A *photograph feature* specifies metadata about the specific circumstances related to the photo, such as how, when and why the photo was taken.
- A *medium feature* represents metadata about the manner in which the photo is stored, including, for example, storage format or resolution.

The subject matter vocabulary acts as a domain-specific ontology used to describe the theme of the photo. It consists of the following four elements:

- an agent (e.g. "an ape"),
- an action (e.g. "eating"),
- an object (e.g. "a banana"), and
- a setting (e.g. "in a forest at dawn").

A more detailed structure of the photo annotation ontology is presented in Fig. 3.9 in the form of a UML class diagram. The white-filled triangle arrow represents the inheritance relation (*"is-kind-of"*). The lines ending with a black diamond represent the composition relations (*"part-of"*).

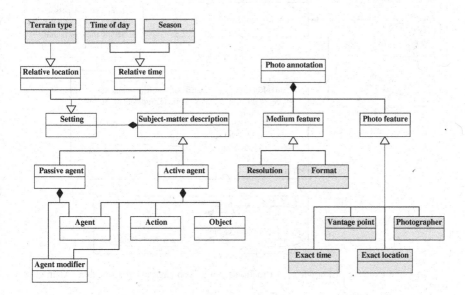

Fig. 3.9 Structure of the photo annotation ontology (Schreiber et al. 2001)

3.3.4 Knowledge Extraction

Knowledge extraction refers to automatically obtaining knowledge from structured or unstructured sources. The obtained knowledge is represented in a formal conceptualized manner according to a formal specification (e.g. an ontology), which enables such knowledge to be used for automated reasoning.

An example of an ontology-based system for extracting knowledge from web pages is Artequakt (Alani et al. 2003). The knowledge extraction process using Artequakt takes place in the following steps (Fig. 3.10a):

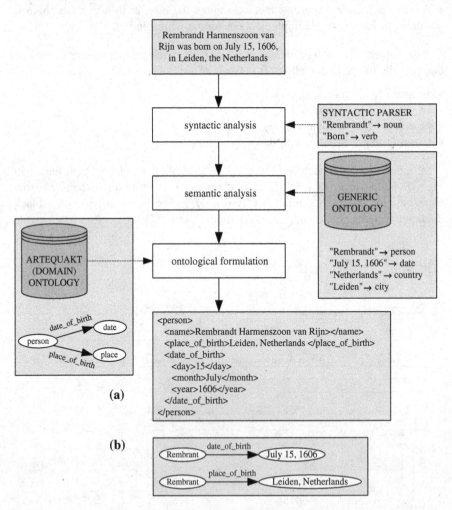

Fig. 3.10 An example of knowledge extraction from a Web page using Artequakt (Alani et al. 2003)

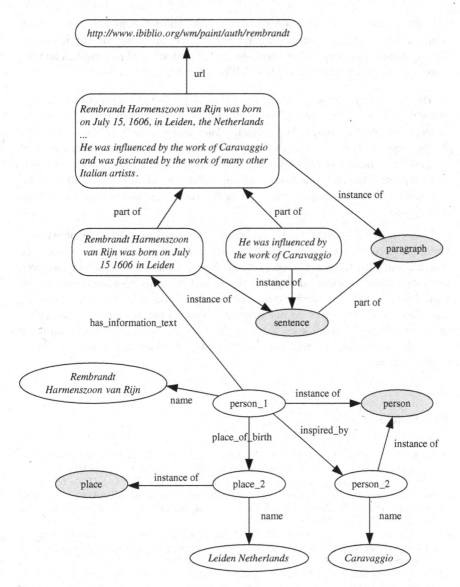

Fig. 3.11 Knowledge base populated with knowledge presented according to the ontology domain representation (Alani et al. 2003)

- In the syntactic analysis, the content of a web page is first divided into paragraphs and sentences, which are then analyzed to determine the grammatical relationships between individual entities.
- Semantic analysis identifies the named entities such as personal and place names, dates, etc. The knowledge needed for such an analysis is obtained from a general-purpose ontology or WordNet.

- In the ontological formulation phase, the semantic relations between pairs of entities are inferred from the domain ontology by matching the entities to the corresponding concepts. The resulting triples consisting of two entities and the associating semantic relation (Fig. 3.10b) are represented in XML.

The knowledge extracted from web pages is presented according to the representation in domain ontology using the relations and the instantiations of the concepts from the ontology. The extracted knowledge represented in such a form is, therefore, suitable for the automatic population of the knowledge base. An example of content from the knowledge base is presented in Fig. 3.11. The gray ovals represent the concepts from ontology, while the white ovals stand for their instantiations (i.e. the entities) representing the knowledge that was extracted from web pages.

This chapter presented various scientific contributions related to ontologies. Ontologies provide a committing set of terms used to represent domain knowledge which is intended to be shared and reused. As such, ontologies can be considered as content theories about the types of things and relations between them that are typical for a specific knowledge domain (Chandrasekaran et al. 1999). On the other hand, however, ontologies do not inherently specify the mechanisms that determine how the represented knowledge should be used in practice. Based on these facts, the next chapter puts ontologies into a broader scope of knowledge representation.

References

Alani H, Kim S, Millard D, Weal M, Hall W, Lewis P, Shadbolt N (2003) Automatic ontology-based knowledge extraction from web documents. IEEE Intell Syst 18(1):14–21

Barforoush AA, Rahnama A (2012) Ontology learning: revisited. J Web Eng 11(4):269–289

Beale S, Nirenburg S, Mahesh K (1995) Semantic analysis in the Mikrokosmos machine translation project. In: Proceedings of the second symposium on natural language processing (SNLP-95), Bangkok, Thailand

Biebow B, Szulman S, Clément A (1999) TERMINAE: a linguistics-based tool for the building of a domain ontology. In: Knowledge acquisition, modeling and management. Lecture notes in computer science, vol 1621. Springer, Berlin, pp 49–66

Blaschke C, Valencia A (2002) Automatic ontology construction from the literature. Genome Inform 13:201–213

Borst WN (1997) Construction of engineering ontologies for knowledge sharing and reuse. Dissertation, Centre for Telematics and Information Technology

Bozsak E, Ehrig M, Handschuh S, Hotho A, Maedche A, Motik B, Oberle D, Schmitz C, Staab S, Stojanovic L, Stojanovic N, Studer R, Stumme G, Sure Y, Tane J, Volz R, Zacharias V (2002) KAON—towards a large scale semantic web. In: E-commerce and web technologies. Lecture notes in computer science, vol 2455. Springer, Berlin, pp 231–248

Brachman RJ, Schmolze J (1985) An overview of the KL-ONE knowledge representation system. Cognitive Sci 9(2):171–216

Chandrasekaran B, Josephson J, Benjamins V (1999) What are ontologies, and why do we need them? IEEE Intell Syst App 14(1):20–26

Chen H, Finin T, Joshi A (2003a) An ontology for context aware pervasive computing environments. Knowl Eng Rev 18(3):197–207

Chen H, Finin T, Joshi A (2003) An intelligent broker for context-aware systems. In: Adjunct proceedings of Ubicomp, Seattle

Common Logic Working Group (2012) Common logic working group documents. http://cl.tamu.edu. Accessed 25 Sep 2012

Dublin Core Metadata Initiative (2012) DCMI Home: Dublin core metadata initiative (DCMI). http://dublincore.org/. Accessed 25 Sep 2012

DogmaModeler (2012) http://www.jarrar.info/Dogmamodeler/. Accessed 25 Sep 2012

Fensel D, Harmelen F, Horrocks I, McGuinness D, Patel-Schneider P (2001) OIL: an ontology infrastructure for the semantic web. IEEE Intell Syst 16(2):38–45

Fortuna B, Grobelnik M, Mladenić D (2007) OntoGen: semi-automatic ontology editor. In: Proceedings of the 2007 conference on human interface, Beijing

Gal A, Modica G, Jamil H (2004) OntoBuilder: fully automatic extraction and consolidation of ontologies from web sources. In: Proceedings of the 20th international conference on data engineering, Boston

Gangemi A, Guarino N, Masolo C, Oltramari A, Schneider L (2002) Sweetening ontologies with DOLCE. In: Knowledge engineering and knowledge management: ontologies and the semantic web. Lecture notes in computer science, vol 2473. Springer, Heidelberg, pp 223–233

Genesereth MR, Fikes RE (1992) Knowledge interchange format, version 3.0, reference manual. Technical report, Computer Science Department, Stanford University

Gomez-Perez A, Corcho O (2002) Ontology languages for the semantic web. IEEE Intell Syst 17(1):54–60

Gruber TR (1993) A translation approach to portable ontology specifications. Knowl Acquis 5(2):199–220

Guarino N (1998) Formal ontology and information systems. In: Proceedings of formal ontology in information systems, Trento, June 1998

Guarino N, Giaretta P (1995) Ontologies and knowledge bases, towards a terminological clarification. In: Mars NJI (ed) Towards very large knowledge bases. IOS Press, Amsterdam, pp 25–32

Guarino N, Welty C (2002) Evaluating ontological decisions with OntoClean. Commun ACM 45(2):61–65

Heflin J, Hendler J, Luke S (1999) SHOE: a knowledge representation language for internet applications. Technical report, University of Maryland

Hozo-Ontology Editor (2012) http://www.hozo.jp/. Accessed 25 Sep 2012

Jaimes A, Smith JR (2003) Semi-automatic, data-driven construction of multimedia ontologies. In: Proceedings of the IEEE international conference on multimedia and expo (ICME), Baltimore, 6–9 July 2003

Jarrar M, Meersman R (2002) Formal ontology engineering in the DOGMA approach. In: Meersman R, Tari Z (eds.) On the move to meaningful internet systems 2002: CoopIS, DOA, and ODBAS. Lecture notes in computer science, vol 2519. Springer, Berlin, pp 1238–1254

KAON2 (2012) KAON2—Ontology management for the semantic web. http://kaon2.semanticweb.org/. Accessed 25 Sep 2012

Karp R, Chaudhri V, Thomere J (1999) XOL: An XML-based ontology exchange language, version 0.4. http://www.ai.sri.com/pkarp/xol/xol.html. Accessed 25 Sep 2012

Khoo C, Na J-C (2006) Semantic relations in information science. Annu Rev Inf Sci Technol 40(1):157–228

Kietz JU, Maedche A, Volz R (2000) A method for semi-automatic ontology acquisition from a corporate intranet. In: Proceedings of the EKAW workshop on ontologies and text, Juan-Les-Pins, Oct 2000

Laboratory for Applied Ontology (2012) DOLCE. http://www.loa.istc.cnr.it/DOLCE.html. Accessed 25 Sep 2012

Lenat DB, Guha RV (1989) Building large knowledge-based systems: representation and inference in the Cyc project. Addison-Wesley Longman, Boston

Liu W, Weichselbraun A, Scharl A, Chang E (2005) Semi-automatic ontology extension using spreading activation. J Univ Knowl Manag 0(1):50–58

MacGregor R, Bates R (1987) The loom knowledge representation language. Technical report ISI/RS-87-188, Information Sciences Institute, University of Southern California

Maedche A, Staab S (2001) Ontology learning for the semantic web. IEEE Intell Syst 16(2):72–79

Mahesh K (1996) Ontology development for machine translation: ideology and methodology. Technical report, Computer Research Laboratory, New Mexico State University

Martin D, Burstein M, Hobbs J, Lassila O, McDermott D, McIlraith S, Narayanan S, Paolucci M, Parsia B, Payne T, Sirin E, Srinivasan N, Sycara K (2004) OWL-S: semantic markup for web services, W3C member submission. http://www.w3.org/Submission/OWL-S/. Accessed 25 Sep 2012

Mizoguchi R, Sunagawa E, Kozaki K, Kitamura Y (2007) A model of roles within an ontology development tool: Hozo. Appl Ontol 2(2):159–179

Navigli R, Velardi P (2004) Learning domain ontologies from document warehouses and dedicated web sites. Comput Linguist 30(2):151–179

Navigli R, Velardi P, Gangemi A (2003) Ontology learning and its application to automated terminology translation. IEEE Intell Syst 18(1):22–31

Noy NF, Sintek M, Decker S, Crubézy M, Fergerson RW (2001) Creating semantic web contents with protege-2000. IEEE Intell Syst 16(2):60–71

OntoClean Central (2012) http://www.ontoclean.org/. Accessed 25 Sep 2012

OpenCyc.org (2012) http://www.opencyc.org/. Accessed 25 Sep 2012

OWL Working Group (2009) OWL 2 web ontology language document overview. W3C recommendation 27 October 2009. http://www.w3.org/TR/owl-overview/. Accessed 25 Sep 2012

The protégé ontology editor and knowledge acquisition system (2012) http://protege.stanford.edu/. Accessed 25 Sep 2012

Schreiber AT, Dubbeldam B, Wielemaker J, Wielinga B (2001) Ontology-based photo annotation. IEEE Intell Syst 16(3):66–74

Schreiber G (2008) Knowledge engineering. In: van Harmelen F, Lifschitz V, Porter B (eds) Handbook of knowledge representation. Elsevier, Amsterdam, pp 929–946

Semafora systems (2012) OntoStudio. http://www.semafora-systems.com/en/products/ontostudio/. Accessed 25 Sep 2012

Studer R, Benjamins VR, Fensel D (1998) Knowledge engineering: principles and methods. Data Knowl Eng 25(1–2):161–197

The Suggested Upper Merged Ontology (SUMO) (2012) Ontology portal. http://www.ontologyportal.org/. Accessed 25 Sep 2012

Sure Y, Studer R (2002) On-to-knowledge methodology. In: Davies J, Fensel D, van Harmelen F (eds) On-to-knowledge: semantic web–enabled knowledge management. Wiley, New York, pp 33–46

TerminaeWiki (2012) http://lipn.univ-paris13.fr/terminae/index.php/Main_Page. Accessed 25 Sep 2012

Weiten M (2009) OntoSTUDIO® as a ontology engineering environment. In: Davies J, Grobelnik M, Mladenic D (eds) Semantic knowledge management: integrating ontology management, knowledge discovery, and human. Springer, Berlin, pp 51–60

Chapter 4
Knowledge Representation

The explanation of the term *knowledge* very often involves using the term *information*. Loosely stated, knowledge is information in support of or in conflict with a certain hypothesis, or it serves to resolve a problem or answer a specific question. Specific knowledge that results from information processing may be either expected or it may be new and surprising. The initially gathered information is often fragmented and unstructured, and in that form it is not suitable for further exchange and processing across different systems. Moreover, one does not usually have an a priori understanding of what the atoms of knowledge are, how they are connected, and how one can retrieve or deduce new knowledge from them. In order to answer some of these important questions, the next section begins by examining different definitions of knowledge, followed by a discussion of knowledge organization, and concluding with practical applications of knowledge representations.

4.1 Definition of Knowledge

Knowledge and *concept* are among the most abstract terms in human vocabulary. Similarly to the term *concept*, all the characteristics of knowledge cannot be captured within a single definition. The ancient philosopher Plato described knowledge as *"justified true belief"*. According to Plato, a person knows a proposition to be true if (and only if) he or she believes in the truth of the proposition and at the same time has justification for doing so. In the following centuries, many definitions and theories of knowledge were proposed; however, not a single one has been widely agreed upon.

Similarly to the definitions of concepts, attempts to define knowledge were also made in other disciplines besides philosophy. These definitions are often tailored to meet the specificities of the field, which also involves the use of specific terminology. For example, from the viewpoint of cognitive psychology, knowledge is considered a *"cognitive subject matter content"* (Merrill 2000). When it comes to computer science, a very pragmatic position towards explaining knowledge is

G. Jakus et al., *Concepts, Ontologies, and Knowledge Representation*,
SpringerBriefs in Computer Science, DOI: 10.1007/978-1-4614-7822-5_4,
© The Author(s) 2013

taken, as it is often considered that knowledge must have an applicable, functional or even predictive value. Such position is reflected also in the following definitions of knowledge from the field of computer science:

- *"Whatever can be ascribed to an agent, such that its behavior can be computed according to the principle of rationality"* (Newell 1982);
- *"Whole body of data and information that people bring to bear to practical use in action, in order to carry out tasks and create new information"* (Schreiber et al. 2000);
- *"Conceptual models of systems and principles"* that explain *"functioning, causes and effects, form, features and may have a predictive nature"* (Halladay and Milligan 2004).

The definition of knowledge is partly demanding because it depends on the context. This can be illustrated, for example, by taking the definition of (Schreiber et al. 2000) which defines knowledge in terms of data and information. It is, however, difficult to make a clear distinction between data (*"the uninterpreted signals that reach our senses"*), information (*"data equipped with meaning"*) and knowledge itself, because such distinction depends on the respective circumstances. In certain situations, one person's knowledge can, namely, represent completely meaningless data for someone else. For example, all knowledge a skilled chess player has on opening strategies makes very little sense to someone who does not know how the individual chess pieces move.

If it is so difficult to define knowledge, why should one take the trouble of defining it? Even without an explicit definition, knowledge can be recognized from observing the activity of entities (human or software agents) that are capable of particular actions, and the effects of such activity (Newell 1982; Guarino and Giaretta 1995; Schreiber et al. 2000). For example, we are able to differentiate between knowledgeable and ignorant people by simply observing their actions to achieve a pursued goal. When, for example, witnessing a person waving around with a computer mouse, one can conclude that he or she does not have the knowledge on how to use this device to interact with the computer.

Despite the diversity of views regarding the nature of knowledge, there seems to be a broader agreement on distinguishing different types of knowledge. The matter was first discussed by philosophers Bertrand Russell distinguishing between *declarative knowledge* and *knowledge by acquaintance* (Russell 1912), and Gilbert Ryle distinguishing between *declarative* and *procedural knowledge* (Ryle 1949).

Declarative knowledge describes facts or the understanding that something is true. Such knowledge can be expressed verbally, for example using declarative sentences, such as *"London hosted the 2012 Summer Olympic Games"*. Declarative knowledge is also referred to as descriptive or propositional knowledge or "knowledge that".

Procedural knowledge, on the other hand, refers to the ability or possession of a skill to perform a task in an efficient way. It may not always be possible to verbalize procedural knowledge, as it can sometimes only be recognized "in action" or by its effect. The difference between declarative and procedural knowledge is, for example, reflected in the ability to swim. You may know how to move arms and legs, but until you actually apply this declarative knowledge in (deep enough) water, you cannot actually consider yourself a swimmer. Procedural knowledge is also referred to as imperative knowledge or "know-how".

Knowledge by acquaintance refers to familiarity with someone or something gained through experience. For example, in order *to know* human feelings such as love or fear, one must experience them first. The meaning of the verb "*to know*" used in the previous sentence refers to knowledge by acquaintance. Knowledge by acquaintance is also referred to as personal knowledge or "knowing of".

The use of knowledge adds a great value to computer systems. However, this introduces the question of how to represent and organize knowledge in a uniform manner to make it suitable for use and sharing. In order to provide answers to this important issue, knowledge representation and organization issues are discussed next.

4.2 Representing and Organizing Knowledge

4.2.1 Knowledge Representation

The term "knowledge representation" refers to "*using formal symbols to represent a collection of propositions believed by some putative agent*" (Brachman and Levesque 2004). As such, knowledge representation acts as an internal representation of reality inside an intelligent agent. As every practical instance of knowledge representation contains only a limited number of propositions about the world, it can only approximate reality and, in addition, it inevitably gives more focus to some things and at the same time neglects others. By choosing a specific type of knowledge representation, the intelligent agent is, therefore, bound to use a specific set of terms which determine how and what to perceive of reality. These terms are also referred to as "ontological commitments" (Davis et al. 1993).

As already discussed in the chapter on ontologies, providing a committing set of terms used to represent reality is, in fact, the task of ontologies. For that reason, ontologies can be considered the heart of every knowledge representation. However, as an actual ontology cannot represent all the propositions about the world (as their number is quite possibly infinite), in most cases, the knowledge contained in an ontology is not sufficient for an intelligent agent to carry out its tasks. To be of practical use for knowledge representation, ontologies therefore must not only serve as a source of explicitly recorded knowledge, but must also provide the means to create new knowledge by manipulating the existing knowledge through a process referred to as *reasoning*.

To establish a basis for reasoning, ontologies must be "embedded" into a suitable framework which includes a formal system of logic and an efficient computational environment (Davis et al. 1993; Sowa 2010). Besides supplying the symbols and formal structure for representation, *logic* also provides the rules and operations that can be used on symbols to create new knowledge through the process of reasoning. *Computational environment* provides the means for computationally efficient reasoning and use of represented knowledge in practical applications.

4.2.1.1 Formalisms for Representing Knowledge

Every day, we exchange our knowledge with each other and with machines. We do not perform this activity by actually exchanging concrete objects with each other or with a machine, but by exchanging surrogate representations. An important role of knowledge representations is, therefore, also to provide a medium for human expression and communication (Davis et al. 1993). The most widespread medium of such type is *natural language*. Although natural languages are very expressive, they are, however, often ambiguous, inconsistent, underspecified and difficult to model, and are as such, therefore, not appropriate to be used for the representation of knowledge and its manipulation within computer systems. For this purpose, other more "computer friendly" formalisms are much more appropriate, for example semantic networks, frames, description logics, conceptual graphs and fuzzy logic.

Semantic networks are graphical structures that are particularly suitable for representing static world knowledge. The nodes in semantic networks represent concepts or objects connected with binary semantic relations acting as graph edges.

Frames are knowledge representation structures influenced by the organization of human memory. A frame is a *"remembered framework"* suitable for representing *"stereotyped situations"* (like, for example, going to a birthday party) (Minsky 1975). A frame consists of the so-called *slots* which can be interpreted as some sort of properties or attributes that can be assigned values or references to other frames. The content of the slots representing facts is fixed, while the content of other slots, also referred to as "terminals", can be customized to meet the circumstances of the reality that is being represented.

Frames can be considered as an evolution of semantic networks. As slots can contain references to other frames, the resulting associations among the frames form a network of nodes (frames) and relations (linking slots). Nevertheless, frames build on classic semantic networks by introducing default slot values and procedures that enable the dynamic assignment of slot values under particular conditions and circumstances. A frame representing knowledge on one of the authors of this survey is shown in Fig. 4.1.

Description logics are a family of knowledge representation languages that can be used to *describe* an application domain through formal, *logic*-based semantics (Baader et al. 2008). By providing the latter, description logics build upon semantic networks and frames. Description logics have good computational properties, which in turn enables efficient reasoning.

slot	value	value type
A kind of	Human	reference to the parent frame
Birthdate	15/4/1982	instance value
Age	*Sum(currentDate(), -Birthdate)*	procedure
Gender	Male	instance value
Number of legs	2	value inherited from parent frame
Number of teeth	28	overridden default value inherited from parent frame

Fig. 4.1 Representing knowledge using a frame

Conceptual graphs (Sowa 1984) are a logical formalism based on existential graphs (Peirce 1909) and semantic networks. Conceptual graphs are used to represent knowledge in a *"logically precise, humanly readable, and computationally tractable"* form that can, in addition, be represented in different notations including human language.

Fuzzy logic is an extension of the traditional logical systems offering the framework for knowledge representation in environments characterized by uncertainty and imprecision. In contrast to other typical approaches to knowledge representation which only enable exact knowledge representation and drawing conclusions based on the latter, fuzzy logic functions in a way that is much more similar to that of the human mind.

4.2.2 Knowledge Organization

When representing knowledge, two basic levels of representation can be recognized corresponding to the content and the structure (or the organization) of knowledge (van Geenen 2004; Stillings et al. 1995). The content of knowledge refers to using formal symbols to represent the concepts of reality. Such content is organized by means of *knowledge structures*. The two levels of knowledge representation can also be looked upon as a distinction between the semantics and the syntax of knowledge representations. While syntax deals with the way of arranging symbols used to represent knowledge (i.e. knowledge structures), semantics addresses the meaning of these symbols and their arrangements (i.e. knowledge content).

The difficulty connected with defining knowledge is to a large extent related to the content of knowledge, as this is domain- and context-dependant. On the other hand, knowledge structures can, in general, be applied to a wide range of domains (Schreiber et al. 2000). Some examples of such knowledge structures are presented in the continuation of this survey.

4.2.2.1 Imitation of Human Memory

Perhaps the most natural approach to the organization of knowledge is to organize it similarly to the way in which it is organized in human memory. As proposed in Merrill (2000), knowledge can be represented by using the so-called *knowledge objects* which consist of *knowledge components*. From this perspective, four types of knowledge objects are essential for organizing knowledge:

- *entities*—representing things or objects;
- *actions*—representing procedures that can be performed on, to or with entities or their parts;
- *processes*—representing the events that occur as a result of an action, and
- *properties*—representing descriptors for entities, actions, or processes.

Knowledge components are, in general, used to name, describe, or illustrate the parent knowledge object or its parts. In addition, knowledge components also define the relations of a knowledge object to the components of other objects. For example, the components of a knowledge object representing a process (or knowledge about how something works) describe:

- the conditions for executing the process (e.g. matching particular property values),
- the outcomes of process execution (e.g. property values that are changed as a result of the process) and
- other processes that are potentially triggered by the respective process.

A generic knowledge structure that can be used to represent a process is illustrated in Fig. 4.2.

The application of the presented model can be explained with (the activity of) illuminating a room. The activity starts by acting on the light switch which serves as a controller of the entity "the light". The entity contains the property "state" with two possible assigned values, i.e. "on" or "off", which can be portrayed, respectively, with a bulb with or without emerging light rays. The value of the property "state" is the condition for the execution of the process of "turning on the light". If the value of this property at the moment of triggering the process on the controller is "on", then the process will not be executed. In the case when the value of the property "state" is "off", the process would alter it to "on". In addition, the process of turning on the light could also trigger another process, for example, turning on another light in the room.

Fig. 4.2 Process knowledge structure (Merrill 2000)

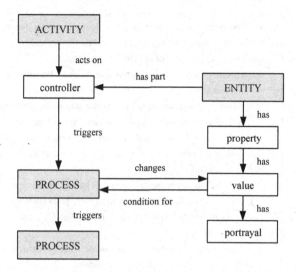

4.2.2.2 WordNet

WordNet was already briefly presented in the chapter on concepts. There we mentioned that this lexical database consists of sets of synonym words, referred to as synsets, which express concepts lexically. Since individual words can have more than one meaning (phenomena referred to as *polysemy*), they can appear in more than one synset. Polysemic relations between the individual senses of a word have an important impact on the structure of WordNet, as they impose the organization of synsets in the form of a semantic network.

However, polysemy is not the only relation that affects the topology of WordNet. By its nature, polysemy links lexical units representing concepts rather than linking concepts directly. The relations among concepts in WordNet are established primarily by arranging the concepts into a hierarchy in which a concept that is subordinate to another concept is considered more specific. As such, it inherits general knowledge from its superordinate concept, so that it only needs to enclose the respective specific knowledge. Such organization of knowledge is influenced by the organization of human semantic memory (Fellbaum 2010), which is in turn similar to the approach presented in the previous section.

In the case of nouns and verbs, the described hierarchy is based on the hypernym relation, where each subordinate concept is "a kind of" its superordinate concept. Figure 4.3 shows the hypernymic hierarchy for the concept *homo*. The synonyms forming a synset are presented in strong text, while their definitions (descriptions) are written in parentheses.

With some proposed ways of characterizing knowledge organization already presented, the following section focuses on various possibilities of knowledge use in intelligent computer systems.

---

homo, man, human being, human -- (any living or extinct member of the family Hominidae characterized by superior intelligence, articulate speech, and erect carriage)

=> **hominid** -- (a primate of the family Hominidae)

  => **primate** -- (any placental mammal of the order Primates; has good eyesight and flexible hands and feet)

    => **placental, placental mammal, eutherian, eutherian mammal** -- (mammals having a placenta; all mammals except monotremes and marsupials)

      => **mammal, mammalian** -- (any warm-blooded vertebrate having the skin more or less covered with hair; young are born alive except for the small subclass of monotremes and nourished with milk)

        => **vertebrate, craniate** -- (animals having a bony or cartilaginous skeleton with a segmented spinal column and a large brain enclosed in a skull or cranium)

          => **chordate** -- (any animal of the phylum Chordata having a notochord or spinal column)

            => **animal, animate being, beast, brute, creature, fauna** -- (a living organism characterized by voluntary movement)

              => **organism, being** -- (a living thing that has (or can develop) the ability to act or function independently)

                => **living thing, animate thing** -- (a living (or once living) entity)

                  => **object, physical object** -- (a tangible and visible entity; an entity that can cast a shadow;)

                    => **physical entity** -- (an entity that has physical existence)

                      => **entity** -- (that which is perceived or known or inferred to have its own distinct existence (living or nonliving))

Fig. 4.3 Example of a hierarchy of synsets from WordNet (Princeton 2010)

4.3 Knowledge Use

The main use of knowledge by humans (Merrill 2000) as well as by software agents (Newell 1982) is, clearly, to support intelligent behavior essential for solving problems. The process of integrating knowledge into computer systems that are designed to imitate problem solving that normally requires human experts is referred to as *knowledge engineering* (Feigenbaum and McCorduck 1983), while the respective systems are known as *knowledge-based systems* (KBS) or *expert systems*.

A typical knowledge-based system consist at least of:

- a *knowledge base* containing organized expert knowledge represented by using one of knowledge representation formalisms; and
- a *reasoning engine* with mechanisms for automated reasoning. The task of the reasoning engine is to derive new conclusions from the knowledge in the knowledge base in order to imitate the problem solving process of a human expert.

4.3.1 Knowledge Acquisition

Successful problem solving requires a high level of expertise. The value of a knowledge-based system is, therefore, closely related to the quality and the extent of knowledge stored in its knowledge base. The process of extracting, structuring and organizing knowledge to be used in knowledge-based systems is referred to as *knowledge acquisition* (Waterman 1985). The aim of knowledge acquisition is to acquire and structure data required for creating a knowledge model intended to be used for automated problem-solving that is expected to provide similar results compared to those provided by domain experts.

It is precisely the latter who are the most valuable source of knowledge. Knowledge acquisition through direct interaction with human experts is referred to as *knowledge elicitation*. Techniques and methods for knowledge elicitation include interviewing, brainstorming, protocols, laddering, observations, sorting, and many others (Medesker et al. 1995; Schreiber et al. 2000). The purpose of these techniques is to acquire different types of knowledge an expert possesses, including the knowledge an expert is not consciously aware of and it is therefore difficult to reach and articulate (Studer et al. 1998). An example of such knowledge is procedural knowledge which is manifested in the respective expert's skills.

Besides obtaining knowledge from human experts, it can also be extracted from digital sources, such as, for example, electronic documents, databases and the internet, by using the techniques of *knowledge discovery*.

4.3.2 Knowledge Modeling

The data gathered in knowledge acquisition are structured and represented, for example, in the form of annotated documents or diagrams. The structured data are first validated and then used to build a knowledge model in a process referred to as *knowledge modeling*. The knowledge model is stored in a knowledge base by using one of the knowledge representation formalisms that enable the knowledge to be interpretable by a reasoning engine.

The main characteristics of knowledge modeling are the following (Studer et al. 1998):

- The process of knowledge modeling is never completed. As the resulting knowledge models only an approximation of the real world, there is always room for further improvement.
- Consequently, knowledge modeling is often carried out in a number of iterations. In each iteration, the current version of the model serves as a starting point for further refinements and modifications or even acquisition of new knowledge.
- Because knowledge modeling is subject to subjective and consequently potentially faulty interpretations of knowledge engineers, the evolving knowledge models should be revised and evaluated with respect to reality in each stage of the process.

Various methodologies for building knowledge models have been proposed. The majority of them focuses on building ontologies, which is why some of them were already listed in the section on ontologies. CommonKADS methodology (Schreiber et al. 2000), an example of a methodology exceeding the scope of ontologies, is presented in the continuation.

The knowledge model described in CommonKADS captures three categories of knowledge required to solve a particular problem: domain knowledge, inference knowledge and task knowledge. In the continuation of this survey, the three categories are described by using an example of a simple medical diagnosis application (Fig. 4.4).

Domain knowledge corresponds to an ontology with domain-specific terms which can be used as a static knowledge base reusable for solving diverse tasks within an application. In the medical diagnosis application, domain knowledge would, for example, include the definitions of symptoms, diseases, and tests to confirm the diseases, and in addition, the relations among the above-mentioned elements.

Inference knowledge describes the reasoning primitives, or *inferences*, that can be used to carry out the reasoning process applied on domain knowledge. The knowledge model of the medical application, presented in Fig. 4.4, includes two such inferences. The inference "hypothesize" relates the observed symptoms with a probable disease, while the inference "verify" determines the tests that are able to confirm whether the specified symptoms are, in fact, caused by the assumed disease.

Task knowledge describes the goals of applying knowledge in the application as well as strategies to accomplish these goals. Such strategies are described with the aid of several levels of decompositions, through which complex tasks are broken-down into more basic tasks which are eventually associated to inferences. Beside the decomposition process, task knowledge also defines the way in which the tasks

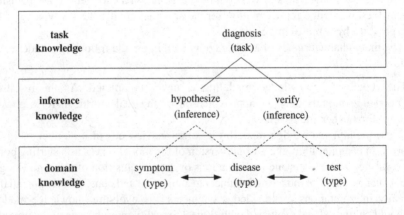

Fig. 4.4 The knowledge model in CommonKADS (Schreiber et al. 2000)

are carried out. The top-level "diagnosis" task of the medical application from Fig. 4.4 can, for example, be carried out by repeatedly invoking the sequence of both inferences from the inference layer.

4.3.3 Reasoning

Once knowledge is acquired, modeled and stored in a knowledge base, it is ready to be used for problem solving. The process of problem solving requires deriving conclusions reached by reasoning over explicitly represented knowledge. Conclusions can be reached by using different methods and strategies, and can thus be supported with different rationales on why a particular conclusion was selected over a wide range of others. In the continuation, the most common types of reasoning are presented, i.e. deduction, induction, abductive reasoning and reasoning by analogy.

Deduction is a type of reasoning which necessarily derives a conclusion from the given premises. If the premises are true, then the conclusions derived from the deduction process are also true. In general, deductive reasoning derives specific conclusions from more general evidence, for example:

Premise 1:   *All men are mortal*
Premise 2:   *Socrates is a man*
Conclusion: *Socrates is mortal*

Induction can be in many ways considered an opposite of deduction. To start with, it is a type of reasoning which draws *general* conclusions based on the abstraction of observations of (many) individual *specific* instances, for example:

Premise 1:   *Socrates is mortal*
Premise 2:   *Socrates is a man*
Conclusion: *All men are mortal*

As opposed to deductive reasoning, inductive reasoning does not guarantee the truth of the conclusions, even if all the premises are true. This can be manifested in the philosophical *problem of induction*, famously illustrated by the historic *black swan problem*:

Premise: *All swans we have seen so far were white*
Conclusion: *All swans are white.* *

This conclusion is, of course, false, since black swans were discovered in the eighteenth century.

Abductive reasoning is a type of reasoning which does not draw certain conclusions but rather yields hypotheses or explanations of observation. As there can be an infinite number of explanations, abductive reasoning attempts to bring forward a single explanation by invalidating alternative explanations.

Abductive reasoning is, for example, very common in medicine. When diagnosing a patient, many possible diseases fit the displayed symptoms, but one of
them is considered as more probable than others.

Analogical reasoning compares specific details of two concepts and concludes
that if the examined concepts are alike in those details, then they can possibly be
alike also in (some of) the others. Analogical reasoning can be considered as a
form of inductive reasoning, as it does not assure the truth of the conclusions but
rather extends, although perhaps inaccurately, our understanding on previously
unknown concepts. This is illustrated in the following example, where (at least if
referring to cartoon characters) the analogical reasoning yields a false conclusion.

Premise 1:   *Tom is a cat and Tom catches mice*
Premise 2:   *Garfield is a cat*
Conclusion: *Garfield catches mice.**

Analogical reasoning derives particular conclusions from particular premises
and in this respect differs from the other three types of reasoning, where at least
one of the propositions is general.

Solving complex problems often requires the application of a combination of
different types of reasoning. Diagnosing a disease in the medical application from
Fig. 4.4, for example, involves an instance of abductive reasoning ("hypothesize")
and an instance of deductive reasoning ("verify"), which is illustrated in Fig. 4.5.

4.3.4 Applications of Knowledge-Based Systems

One of the common uses of knowledge-based systems is to provide non-professional users professional guidance when it is difficult to provide the actual support
of an expert. The user interacts with a knowledge-based system (KBS) through a
user interface which allows the user to issue queries to the KBS, answer additional
questions asked by the KBS and receive solutions or advice (Fig. 4.6).

Knowledge-based systems are currently used to assist the users in many fields,
for example in:

- strategy games. (A good example demonstrating the power of knowledge when
  used alongside the processing power of a machine is computer chess. The
  knowledge base of a chess game contains the strategies and moves that can be
  used to simulate the opposing "expert" player. Today, only few people can win
  against the computer in chess, and they can only succeed by taking advantage of
  the knowledge on how computer plans its next moves.);
- recommender systems, for example, recommending movies (Movielens 2012;
  (IMDb 2012), songs (Last.fm 2012; Pandora 2012) and shopping items (Ama-
  zon 2012) or suggesting social connections (Facebook 2012; LinkedIn 2012);

Fig. 4.5 Using a
combination of different
types of reasoning for
problem solving

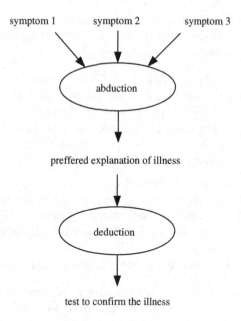

Fig. 4.6 The general
structure of a knowledge-
based system

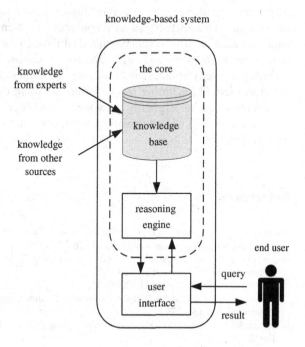

- interactive applications (answering engines (Wolfram 2012), virtual interactive assistants (Siri 2012), tutorial applications (Hatzilygeroudis and Prentzas 2004), etc.).

The use of knowledge-based systems is not limited to the facilitation of tasks of non-professional users, but may also be used to support expert work. This is especially useful in the fields where vast knowledge is required to solve a problem and/or many combinations of input variables (observations) are common, which can lead to seemingly unpredictable conclusions. Such fields, for example, include:

- various kinds of diagnoses, for example machine fault diagnosis, e.g. (Jain et al. 2008), and medical diagnosis, e.g. (Miller et al. 1982);
- complex decision support systems, for example in industrial production, e.g. (Manohar et al. 1999), and agricultural production, e.g. (Cohen and Shoshany 2002); and
- finance, for example in financial analysis (Matsatsinis et al. 1997).

A more extensive review of knowledge-based systems methodologies and applications can be found in (Liao 2005).

The final goal of every application of knowledge, regardless of the nature of the agents using it (be it human or software), is solving some sort of a problem. This chapter presented the most important topics related to the use of knowledge by software agents with the goal of autonomous problem solving. The topics presented focused on how to achieve this goal through the definitions of knowledge, various representations and organizations of knowledge acquired from human experts and other resources, and modeling the acquired knowledge in order to be stored and reused for further manipulation. By using different types of reasoning, the manipulation of explicitly presented knowledge produces new knowledge which is required in order to answer a particular question or, in general, to solve a specific problem.

References

Amazon.com (2012) Amazon.com: online shopping for electronics, apparel, computers, books, DVDs & more.www.amazon.com/. Accessed 25 Sep 2012
Apple (2012) iPhone 4S—Ask Siri to help you get things done. http://www.apple.com/iphone/features/siri.html. Accessed 25 Sep 2012
Baader F, Horrocks I, Sattler U (2008) Description logics. In: van Harmelen F et al (eds) foundations of artificial intelligence. Handbook of knowledge representation, vol 3. Elsevier, Amsterdam, pp 135–179
Brachman RJ, Levesque HJ (2004) Knowledge representation and reasoning. Morgan Kaufmann, Los Altos
Cohen Y, Shoshany M (2002) A national knowledge-based crop recognition in Mediterranean environment. Int J Appl Earth Obs Geoinf 4(1):75–87

Davis R, Shrobe H, Szolovits P (1993) What is a knowledge representation? Artif Intell Mag 14(1):17–33

Facebook (2012) http://www.facebook.com/. Accessed 25 Sep 2012

Feigenbaum EA, McCorduck P (1983) The fifth generation: artificial intelligence and Japan's computer challenge to the world. Addison-Wesley Publishing, Reading

Fellbaum C (2010) WordNet. In: Poli R et al (eds) Theory and applications of ontology: computer applications, Springer Science+Business Media B.V., pp 231–243

Guarino N, Giaretta P (1995) Ontologies and knowledge bases, towards a terminological clarification. In: Mars NJI (ed) Towards very large knowledge bases. IOS Press, Amsterdam, pp 25–32

Halladay S, Milligan C (2004) The application of network science principles to knowledge simulation. In: Proceedings of the 37th annual Hawaii international conference on system sciences, Big Island, 5–8 Jan 2004

Hatzilygeroudis I, Prentzas J (2004) Using a hybrid rule-based approach in developing an intelligent tutoring system with knowledge acquisition and update capabilities. Expert Syst Appl 26(4):477–492

IMDb (2012) Movies, TV and celebrities. http://www.imdb.com/. Accessed 25 Sep 2012

Jain MB, Srinivas MB, Jain A (2008) A novel web based expert system architecture for on-line and off-line fault diagnosis and control (FDC) of transformers. In: Proceedings of the TENCON 2008—2008 IEEE region 10 conference, Hyderabad, 19–21 Nov 2008

Last.fm (2012) http://www.last.fm/. Accessed 25 Sep 2012

Liao S-H (2005) Expert system methodologies and applications—a decade review from 1995 to 2004. Expert Syst Appl 28(1):93–103

LinkedIn (2012) World's largest professional network | LinkedIn. http://www.linkedin.com/. Accessed 25 Sep 2012

Manohar PA, Shivathaya SS, Ferry M (1999) Design of an expert system for the optimization of steel compositions and process route. Expert Syst Appl 17(2):129–134

Matsatsinis NF, Doumpos M, Zopounidis C (1997) Knowledge acquisition and representation for expert systems in the field of financial analysis. Expert Syst Appl 12(2):247–262

Medesker L, Tan M, Turban E (1995) Knowledge acquisition from multiple experts: problems and issues. Expert Syst Appl 9(1):35–40

Merrill MD (2000) Knowledge objects and mental models. In: Proceedings of the international workshop on advanced learning technologies, Palmerston, 12 Apr–12 June, pp 244–246

Miller RA, Pople HE Jr, Myers JD (1982) Internist-1, an experimental computer-based diagnostic consultant for general internal medicine. N Engl J Med 307(8):468–476

Minsky M (1975) A Framework for representing knowledge. In: Winston PH (ed) The psychology of computer vision. McGraw-Hill, New York, pp 211–277

Movielens (2012) Movielens—movie recommendations. http://movielens.umn.edu/. Accessed 25 Sep 2012

Newell A (1982) The knowledge level. Artif Intell 18(1):87–127

Pandora Internet Radio (2012) http://www.pandora.com/. Accessed 25 Sep 2012

Peirce CS (1909) Existential graphs, manuscript 514. http://www.jfsowa.com/peirce/ms514.htm. Accessed 25 Sep 2012

Princeton University (2010) About WordNet. http://wordnet.princeton.edu. Accessed 25 Sep 2012

Russell B (1912) The problems of philosophy. Home University Library, London

Ryle G (1949) The concept of mind. Hutchinson Press, London

Schreiber G, Akkermans H, Anjewierden A, de Hoog R, Shadbolt N, Van de Velde W, Wielinga B (2000) Knowledge engineering and management: the CommonKADS methodology. MIT Press, Cambridge

Sowa JF (1984) Conceptual structures: information processing in mind and machine. Addison-Wesley Publishing, Reading

Sowa JF (2010) Ontology. http://www.jfsowa.com/ontology/index.htm. Last update 29 Nov 2010. Accessed 25 Sep 2012

Stillings NA, Weisler SW, Chase CH, Feinstein MH, Garfield JL, Rissland EL (1995) Cognitive
    science: an introduction, 2nd edn. MIT Press, Cambridge
Studer R, Benjamins VR, Fensel D (1998) Knowledge engineering: principles and methods. Data
    Knowl Eng 25(1–2):161–197
van Geenen E (2004) Knowledge structures and the usability of knowledge systems. Eburon
    Uitgeverij, Delft
Waterman DA (1985) A guide to expert systems. Addison-Wesley Publishing, Reading
Wolfram Research (2012) Wolfram|Alpha: computational knowledge engine. http://
    www.wolframalpha.com/. Accessed 25 Sep 2012

Chapter 5
Trends and Outlook

In the past, the field of knowledge representation already exceeded the academic and research spheres and emerged in practical use as well. Moreover, it also extended beyond the field of its origin, i.e. artificial intelligence, into other fields of computer science. One of the important factors that stimulated the thriving of ontologies in particular was World Wide Web, especially its recent evolution, the so-called Semantic Web. The idea of Semantic Web is consistent with some of the basic goals of knowledge representation. The vision of Semantic Web is to enable semantic interoperability and machine interpretability of data sets from various sources and to provide the mechanisms that enable such data to be used to support the user in an automated and intelligent way.

On the other hand, Semantic Web gives the impression of a deviation from the typical methods of knowledge representation, as it is characterized by a much larger number of data or knowledge sets and agents involved in the processes. In addition to its comprehensiveness, Semantic Web is also characterized by its openness, as it is, in contrast to traditional knowledge representation systems that are mostly available only in a closed laboratory environments, available to virtually everybody. The comprehensiveness and openness of Semantic Web also open several issues in the field of knowledge representation that will have to be addressed in the future and amplify the significance of attending to existing issues. As the majority of trends and challenges in the field of knowledge representation are connected with Semantic Web, the present chapter focuses on this area.

The comprehensiveness of World Wide Web and consequently the available knowledge respectively facilitate the problem of ontology learning. Traditional knowledge acquisition with a limited number of highly qualified experts is extremely time-consuming, which is why recently semi-automatic knowledge acquisition emerged based on the content of voluntary collaborative web projects. In this respect, the most useful type of data appears to be the semi-structured data available, for example, in online encyclopedias, such as Wikipedia (Nastase and Strube 2008), or the content recorded in a structured form that is computer-intelligible (Uchida et al. 1999; Jakus et al. 2012). Completely automated knowledge acquisition from a large number of unstructured documents with the

G. Jakus et al., *Concepts, Ontologies, and Knowledge Representation*,
SpringerBriefs in Computer Science, DOI: 10.1007/978-1-4614-7822-5_5,
© The Author(s) 2013

aid of natural language understanding techniques is, in most cases, not usable in practice, as the results often prove to be unacceptable as regards the quality of the conceptual structures formed in the process. In order to establish a completely automated knowledge acquisition in the future, advances must be made both in the fields of natural language understanding and techniques of machine learning (Antoniou and van Harmelen 2004; Davies et al. 2006).

The next generation of semantic applications will thus be characterized by the acquisition of knowledge from several sources instead of acquiring it from merely one source covering all the needs of target applications. Similar trends can also be expected in the use of knowledge available in existing ontologies. As it is not likely for a single ontology to satisfy all the needs of a certain application, the trends nowadays move towards ontology integration (also known as ontology alignment, matching or mapping). Integrating ontologies is one of the most complex and at the same time most important issues related to the practical implementation of Semantic Web. Consequently, the trend of integrating ontologies has lately gained substantial attention also in the research spheres and has actually become one of the most active fields of research (see for example (Shvaiko and Euzenat 2008)). Although the results are very encouraging, so far integrated ontologies cannot be used in practice in most cases (Antoniou and van Harmelen 2004; Cimiano et al. 2006). Among several challenges connected with the representation of knowledge acquired from several distributed sources, we would like to point out the following issues as stated in (van Harmelen 2002; Antoniou and van Harmelen 2004; Davies et al. 2006; Schubert 2006):

- Due to the integration of knowledge from different sources, one of the challenges is ensuring a homogenous conceptualization of domains, as the contents of individual ontologies are very diverse and their vocabularies inhomogeneous, not to mention the differences in the quality of the presented knowledge.
- A substantial part of the Web is changing faster than traditional knowledge representation techniques can withstand. Problems can occur already when addressing the individual representations, as the missing links between data can cause a shortfall in the distributed knowledge base.
- In traditional knowledge representation, the statements recorded in the knowledge base are almost always considered correct. When a knowledge base is formed from several distributed parts with different administration, questions regarding trust, reputation, integrity and origin must be addressed.
- An important challenge is also the ontology evolution, i.e. the updating of ontologies due to the changes in the domain conceptualization. As certain ontologies are bound to evolve, most ontologies on a global scale will be mutually inconsistent. This is the exact reason why a very clear analysis of the relationships between the individual ontologies in networks and the determination of a formal model of network ontologies are required. The latter must support the evolution of network ontologies and must, in the case of any changes in one of the ontologies, ensure at least a partial consistency.

- In practice, the term "ontology" stands for the conceptual structures of different semantic depths: from common hierarchies and taxonomies to structures with extensive semantic features. In order to be able to support the trend of more and more complex, personalized and intelligent applications, future trends shall require a change from using "surface" conceptual structures to the use of structures with a richer semantic content. The reason for this trend lies in the fact that only the latter can support the use of effective reasoning methods and will allow a more efficient use of web sources for the acquisition of new knowledge.

In general, most attention in the field of knowledge representation is given to the development of ontologies as the conceptualizations of the real world, while the development of the mechanisms of their use often lags behind. In the future, more attention will have to be given to the standardization and implementation of efficient mechanisms for the use of knowledge gathered in ontologies. The issues that have to be addressed according to (van Harmelen 2002; Antoniou and van Harmelen 2004; Brewster and O'Hara 2004; Schubert 2006), are the following:

- One of the very important challenges in the field of knowledge representation is the development of ontologies and the mechanisms of their use with the goal of changing the ontologies into a base for reasoning (and not only the data models or data structures shared among applications). One of the conditions required for this goal to actually be reached is the development of sound and complete reasoning engines. The complexity of the development of reasoning engines with the afore-mentioned features, however, mostly depends on the expressiveness of the language used to record ontologies.
- In the case of Semantic Web, the traditional ideal of sound and complete reasoning must be abandoned, as this is almost impossible due to the complexity of the Web and the diversity of the data sources. The actual level of soundness and completeness of reasoning will mostly depend on the availability of appropriate sources. In most cases, the conclusions will be merely approximations, whereby the reasoning engine shall, at best, also provide the evaluation of the quality of the approximation.
- Typically, a knowledge base is constructed with regards to the purpose of its use. As the purpose of the Semantic Web ontologies can often be unpredictable, more attention will need to be given to developing knowledge representations that will be more task-independent.
- An important challenge is also the development of query and reasoning mechanisms that could be used with a large number of distributed ontologies, in the case of potential inconsistencies between individual ontologies, with limited resources, such as memory, storage space and network latency, and that would be able to make sound compromises between the resource use and the quality of the results.
- As automatic reasoning can be based on knowledge from an unknown source, more attention will need to be given to the development of justification mechanisms and the verification of the conclusions acquired with this process.

- One of the future challenges is also the development of the methods of uncertain, statistic or speculative reasoning (e.g. analogical or abductive reasoning). Despite the fact that such reasoning does not necessarily ensure correct conclusions, it is much more similar to the way people think and solve problems.

To conclude, we would like to point out a very important research field, key to the development of artificial intelligence and information and communication technologies in the future. We refer to the development of autonomous systems that would be able to perform various complex tasks in dynamic environments and would also possess context awareness of their actions (Antoniou and van Harmelen 2004). The expression "context awareness" stems from the field of ubiquitous computing and describes the ability of detection and reaction to the changes in the immediate environment of a certain computer system.

Knowledge representation holds one of the key roles in the development of context awareness. The ontologies offer a viewpoint on a specific domain, with the former being the result of a consensus of a group of interested users put into a specific context. In the future, mechanisms need to be developed that will tailor ontologies to the needs of specific users in their actual context. The challenges in this field comprise of the formal presentation of the context, the determination of the formal relationships between different contexts of ontology use, the development of mechanisms for the selection of the appropriate context in a given situation and reasoning based on context (Davies et al. 2006). The development of reasoning based on context is especially important for user profiling, application personalization and mobility support. The examples of applications including the afore-mentioned areas are nowadays very popular social networks.

To summarize, the results achieved in the domain of knowledge representation so far seem tentative and incomplete. Much work remains to be done. It is expected that under the auspices of Semantic Web and other accompanying concepts and visions, such as intelligent and personalized content retrieval, cloud computing, ubiquitous computing and, last but not least, artificial intelligence, the development of the field will continue.

References

Antoniou G, van Harmelen F (2004) A semantic web primer. MIT press, Cambridge

Brewster C, O'Hara K (2004) Knowledge representation with ontologies: the present and future. IEEE Intell Syst 19(1):72–81

Cimiano P, Völker J, Studer R (2006) Ontologies on demand? a description of the state-of-the-art, applications, challenges and trends for ontology learning from text. Inf Wissenschaft und Praxis 57(6–7):315–320

Davies J, Studer R, Warren P (2006) Semantic web technologies: trends and research in ontology-based systems. Wiley, Chichester

Jakus G, Sodnik J, Tomazic S (2012) The design of E-speranto—a computer language for recording multilingual texts on the web. J Web Eng 11(4):269–289

Nastase V, Strube M (2008) Decoding Wikipedia categories for knowledge acquisition. In: Proceedings of the 23rd national conference on artificial intelligence, vol 2, pp 1219–1224

Schubert L (2006) Turing's dream and the knowledge challenge. In: Proceedings of the national conference on artificial intelligence, vol 21, No 2, Boston, pp 1534–1538

Shvaiko P, Euzenat J (2008) Ten challenges for ontology matching. On the move to meaningful internet systems: OTM 2008, Monterrey. Springer, Berlin, pp 1164–1182

Uchida H, Zhu M, Della Senta T (1999) Universal networking language: a gift for a millennium. The United Nations University, Tokyo

van Harmelen F (2002) How the semantic web will change KR: challenges and opportunities for a new research agenda. Knowl Eng Rev 17(1):93–96